Advance Praise for
The Psilocybin Sessions

"Heather Lee is the real deal, as I have learned by interviewing her twice on my internet radio program, *Mind Body Health & Politics*. Professionally, she is a licensed psychedelic guide; personally, she is a cancer survivor; and refreshingly, she talks about both quite openly. For those wanting to learn about authentic women and the use of psychedelic mushrooms—for personal growth and consciousness expansion—this is a book to read and have in your library to show others. For those seeking their first psychedelic-assisted therapy experience, the trip to join Heather on one of her retreats or for a private session is worth the investment in time, energy, and money."

— **Richard Louis Miller, MA, PhD**
Clinical Psychologist and Author of
Master Your Mind: Practical Tools to Calm Anxiety,
Silence Your Inner Critic and Stop Overthinking

"One of the most important voices in psychedelics today, Heather's mindful way to hold space and share it through inspiring stories, current research, and practical applications holds ground-breaking potential for healing and transformation with psilocybin. I am recommending this book to all my clients!"

— **Lauren Alderfer, PhD**
Author of *Mindful Microdosing:*
A Guidebook and Journal

"You'll cry and smile with joy as you read these moving stories, recognizing pieces of yourself within them. The author's gift is her ability to draw you into each journey—to feel the pain, the release, and the profound renewal that follows. Too often, psychedelic integration, the true backbone of healing, is left unexplored. Heather Lee illuminates integration with uncommon clarity, warmth, and rare insight."

— **Christine Caldwell**
Founder and Executive Director,
End of Life Psychedelic Care

"Anyone curious about how psychedelics could help them alleviate suffering or grow spiritually can benefit from these stories of women's lived experiences with psilocybin. Heather eloquently uses her expert insight and scientific research to explain different ways this plant medicine tailors its magic effects to each individual. The women's deeply personal and moving stories reveal what the psychedelic journey can be like and encourages readers to be open to where it can take them."

— **Elinor Fish**
CEO of Open Air Consulting,
Founder of Run Wild Retreats

"Heather A. Lee has masterfully shared a deeply mindful and personal approach to healing that illuminates the compassionate art of psilocybin-assisted therapy. With authenticity and wisdom, she invites readers into a space where science, spirit, and self-discovery meet. *The Psilocybin Sessions* offers both practitioners and seekers a grounded and personal perspective on the transformative potential of plant medicine from a trusted therapist and guide. This book is an inspiring contribution to the evolving conversation around compassion, awareness, and the healing power within us all."

— Brian Wexler, PhD
Clinical and Health Psychologist,
Founder, Palm Springs Psychedelic Society

THE
Psilocybin Sessions

REAL-LIFE STORIES OF WOMEN'S
WISDOM AWAKENING WITH
PSYCHEDELIC MEDICINE

HEATHER A. LEE, LCSW
Licensed Psychedelic Psychotherapist

FOREWORD BY LISA LING

Modern Wisdom Press
Crestone, Colorado, USA
www.ModernWisdomPress.com

Copyright © Heather Lee, 2025

All rights reserved. No part of this publication may be reproduced or transmitted in any form or by any means, mechanical or electronic, including photocopying or recording, or by any information storage and retrieval system, or transmitted by email, without permission in writing from the author. Reviewers may quote brief passages in reviews.

DISCLAIMER

This book is intended for educational and informational purposes only. It does not constitute medical advice, diagnosis, or treatment. Individuals considering the use of any psychedelic substance should undergo appropriate medical and psychological screening and consult with qualified healthcare professionals.

The stories shared in this book are based on actual experiences of the author's clients. These experiences took place in non-ordinary states of consciousness and are, as such, recounted by the author as the witness and reporter of these experiences. Identifying details have been changed or omitted to protect the privacy and confidentiality of those involved. Each person whose story is included has provided informed consent for their experiences to be shared in this manner.

All sessions described in the book took place in locations where personal psilocybin use was legal or decriminalized, including but not limited to Jamaica, Portugal, Mexico, the Netherlands, and Colorado. The author's role in these sessions was solely as a harm-reduction support person, sitting with individuals as they engaged in their own personal and legal use of psilocybin. Neither the author nor the publisher encourages or advises readers to participate in any illegal activities involving psychedelic substances.

The suggestions for integration practices presented in this book are based on current research and best practices in the field of psychedelic integration. These recommendations are general in nature and are intended to benefit readers seeking to support their own exploration of mystical experiences.

Published 2025

ISBNs: 978-1-951692-59-9 (paperback)
978-1-951692-60-5 (eBook)

Cover design by Karen Polaski
Author photos courtesy of Allison Mae Photography

To the amazing women I've had the honor of supporting on your psilocybin journeys.

Thank you for allowing me to share your stories, healing, and magic with the world.

CONTENTS

Foreword *11*
Introduction *13*

CHAPTER 1   Cancer and My Call to Consciousness 17
CHAPTER 2   A Lick of Healing 29
CHAPTER 3   Rising from the Ashes 41
CHAPTER 4   Inviting Your Inner Child Home 53
CHAPTER 5   Breaking Chains 63
CHAPTER 6   The Missing Piece for Peace 75
CHAPTER 7   Taking a Quantum Leap 85
CHAPTER 8   Remembering the Light of Love 97
CHAPTER 9   Navigating the Darkness 109
CHAPTER 10 Consciously Coming to the End of Life 123
CHAPTER 11 The Portal to
                    Awakening Wisdom and Healing 135

About the Author *139*
Acknowledgments *141*
Glossary *143*
Appendix:
Considerations for Your Psilocybin Medicine Journey *147*
Additional Resources *151*
Endnotes *155*
Thank You *159*

FOREWORD

When I first met Heather Lee, I was struck by her calm presence—an energy that felt both grounded and illuminated. I featured her in a segment for *CBS Mornings* as part of my "Psychedelic Renaissance" series, which explored how ancient plant medicines are being rediscovered and reframed in modern therapeutic contexts. Heather's work stood out not because it was sensational, but because it was deeply human. She wasn't just talking about psilocybin as a molecule or a medical breakthrough; she was talking about women—about healing, remembering, and coming home to themselves.

One year later, I sought out Heather's services to work with my 78-year-old mother, an immigrant from Taiwan who had been harboring decades of trauma in her body, which I believe was manifesting in pain and disease. What unfolded was profound. My mother—a woman who had lived through abandonment, abuse, and loss—found herself reconnecting with a part of her spirit that had been quiet for decades. She has emerged radiant, lighter…and most surprisingly, joyful.

Watching her transformation affirmed what Heather had shared with me: This work isn't about escaping life; it's about meeting it more fully.

Heather Lee is one of the pioneering therapists who has helped shape the growing field of psychedelic-assisted healing. But what makes her work extraordinary is her devotion to the feminine soul—her understanding that women's wisdom, intuition, and connection to nature are integral to our collective healing. *The Psilocybin Sessions* is not a clinical manual or a data-driven defense of psychedelics. It's a collection of sacred stories—real women's journeys into the deepest parts of themselves, guided by a medicine that has been used by indigenous cultures for millennia.

Reading these stories feels like being invited into a circle—a place where women gather, share their truths, and listen with their whole beings. These are stories of grief, courage, awakening, and transformation. They remind us that healing is not linear, and that sometimes the answers we seek live beyond the limits of reason and within the mystery of the heart.

As someone who has spent much of my career telling human stories—stories of resilience, struggle, and grace—I believe that *The Psilocybin Sessions* offers something rare and vital: an honest, reverent exploration of the ways in which psychedelics can help us remember who we truly are. Heather invites us not to believe blindly in the magic of mushrooms, but to trust the magic that already lives within us.

For my mother, that trust opened a door to joy she hadn't felt in years. For me, it reaffirmed the power of storytelling—of women's voices rising together to illuminate what has too long been kept in the shadows.

May this book be a light on your own path back to wonder, wisdom, and wildness.

— **Lisa Ling**

INTRODUCTION

Ordinary Women, Extraordinary Experiences

> We are all filled with longing for the wild. There is a wild woman inside each of us.
>
> — CLARISSA PINKOLA ESTÉS

I believe in magic. I think it's important you know that from the very beginning. I believe that psilocybin mushrooms invite us to step through the door into a realm of consciousness that holds a powerful and eternal mystery.

My three decades as a licensed clinical social worker and my work as one of the first certified and licensed psychedelic-assisted psychotherapists in the United States have taught me much about the human experience. But even more than clinical training or evidence-based practice, I have come to trust in the unseen. I know, without needing proof, that there are realms that science cannot explain. There are places and spaces where medicine meets magic.

As a psychotherapist, my life's work has been rooted in understanding the inner landscapes of women's lives. Over the years, I've come to recognize that beneath the surface of our everyday awareness lies a wellspring of wisdom waiting to be accessed. When I support women in psilocybin sessions, I do so in sacred partnership with the woman, with her inner wisdom, and with the deeper intelligence of the fungi themselves. Psilocybin invites a woman to journey beyond the limits of her conscious mind and into the spaciousness of her soul, where insight, healing, and profound remembering can unfold.

The transformations I've witnessed cannot be measured with charts and graphs. They are psycho-spiritual, alchemical, and sacred. With each woman's healing comes an awakening, a remembrance of who she truly is. Perhaps this moment in psychedelic history, often called the renaissance, is also a return of women's wisdom, rising through the cracks of a world in need of re-enchantment.

Many of the women I've guided on psilocybin journeys describe a sense of coming home to a part of themselves they had forgotten—a part that feels deeply, notices synchronicities, hears the whispers of intuition, and remembers how to navigate life with a deep trust and courage. For many, psilocybin is not just medicine; it's a mirror, a guide, a sacred portal to their soul.

This book is a love letter to the mystery—to psilocybin, to the natural world, and to the sacred wisdom that lies within us all.

It is time for us to remember, reclaim, and reconnect with all that is wise, wonderful, and woven for our healing—and the healing of us all. The plants are speaking. The mushrooms are teaching. And we are finally awakening.

This book touches on the science of psychedelic medicine, but more importantly, you will read the sacred stories of real women I've had the honor to support as they journeyed inward with the ancient medicine of psilocybin mushrooms. These women remind us that when you create space to listen deeply and trust yourself, you can access profound inner wisdom and a magic that often lies quietly beneath the noise of your life.

The women in the stories ahead experienced inspiring journeys of healing. Their stories cover issues you may experience in your own life—grief, anxiety, loss, cancer, and relationship pain. You will follow each woman through her unique psilocybin journey and discover how this medicine experience transforms and transmutes pain and past patterns into power and new perspectives. You will be invited into the mystery of non-ordinary consciousness and the unique wisdom that whispers in this luminal space.

As you read about their transformations, I invite you to step into the mystery and medicine of the mushroom journeys. Let go of what you think you know. Open yourself to the possibility that there is wonder all around you. I hope these stories remind you of the times you have felt and experienced magic, and that they ignite your passion to reconnect with your inner wisdom and intuition in whatever way is right for you.

These stories may also provide you with new paths and perspectives for navigating difficult experiences in your own life. The wisdom these women gleaned on their psychedelic medicine journeys is wisdom for us all. The challenges and decisions they have faced are ones that likely touch many of our lives.

Each chapter offers an opportunity to explore and grow through some of these universal experiences and the wisdom received from "the other side." These journeys are not about escaping reality, but about expanding it and exploring it beyond your ordinary senses. Psilocybin has a way of softening the rigid walls you've built around yourself, offering glimpses into the vastness of your inner worlds and the interconnectedness of all life.

To make the book practical for you, I've included suggestions for integration practices and journaling prompts at the end of each chapter. These can help deepen your learning and foster change to release old patterns, embrace new ways of being, and connect more intentionally with your own inner wisdom.

Just as you would prepare for any voyage, if you're considering embarking upon a psilocybin medicine journey, it's important to properly educate yourself on the experience and its risks and rewards. Please see the appendix in the back of the book for important preparatory and safety considerations before undertaking this work with a properly trained therapist or facilitator.

I welcome and invite you into the circle of women gathered here in these stories to explore your own inner landscapes and the realms beyond the known.

CHAPTER 1

Cancer and My Call to Consciousness

> A woman who knows how to listen to the whispers of her soul will never again be lost in the noise of the world.
>
> — UNKNOWN

Life, at its essence, is really just a journey. Even though you carry a map tucked away in your pocket, it is easy to lose your way in this big, crazy world. Sometimes you stumble into the dense woods of doubt, despair, or disconnection. That's when you need a guide—someone like me to help you look at your map and assess where you've been, where you are, and where you are going.

My path to the work I do today—supporting women with psilocybin (also known as plant medicine) makes perfect sense when I look back over my shoulder. As a child, I ran wild in the woods with a close pack of neighborhood kids. We built forts, dammed rivers, gathered berries, and created an entire wild village. My role in our little tribe was that of the healer. I discovered a succulent plant that soothed stings and nettle rashes, and kids would come to me with their scraped knees and bug bites.

Later in my college years, I was introduced to psilocybin and knew immediately it was a powerful tool for bringing me into a deeper connection with nature and my spirituality. During my master's degree training, I worked with Native American students and learned much about indigenous paths and perspectives on plant medicine. It feels inevitable that 50 years later, I would become one of the first certified and licensed psychedelic-assisted psychotherapists in the United States, leading psilocybin experiences as Medicine Woman Retreats. The path to my future was a trail through the woods of my past.

After training to become a clinical social worker at Arizona State University, I developed a practice that focused on helping people access their own inner healing, their own inner compass, and their own timeless wisdom. I have always been drawn to study and practice modalities that honor and access non-ordinary states of consciousness for healing, such as dreamwork, guided imagery, Shamanic journeying, breathwork, and past-life regression, along with paranormal, humanistic, and transpersonal psychology.

In 2022, I came across an ad to enroll in one of the nation's first psychedelic medicine training programs for mental health professionals. This year-long intensive training program offered by the Integrative Psychiatry Institute started me on a new path to a familiar place. I experienced an inner knowing that this path would always be there waiting for me across time. I enrolled in the first cohort of one of the nation's most reputable training programs to become a certified psychedelic-assisted psychotherapist in the state of Colorado.

A few years later, I became the 22nd mental health professional to become a licensed natural medicine clinical facilitator in the state of Colorado. This extensive training immersed me in all the aspects of using psychedelic medicine as a mental health modality. I had the privilege of attending lectures by the lead researchers at Johns Hopkins, New York University, and Imperial College London. My passion and excitement about this field had me feeling like I was plugged into a high-voltage energy field.

On a Monday in July 2022, I completed the final exam of my year-long psychedelic therapy certification training. That day was a real high. My husband and I had planned a big trip to travel Europe to celebrate this next chapter in our lives. The very next day, that high came crashing down. I got a call from my doctor's office that my breast biopsy had come back positive for cancer.

And so my journey began.

MY JOURNEY

There are times in life when events collide, and you know immediately that it is not a coincidence but something predestined and powerful. You feel it at a visceral, gut level; things almost feel surreal in these moments.

Many women speak of illness as the moment their true healing began—not with medication alone, but with the excavation of suppressed emotions, ancestral grief, or unlived truths. This is exactly how my cancer diagnosis impacted me and informed my path of becoming a psychedelic therapist for women's health and wellness. The timing of my diagnosis seemed cosmically linked to my training. It felt like the universe was handing me a very clear assignment to understand the role psilocybin might play for me in navigating my cancer journey.

I enlisted a friend, who was also a therapist, to come and support me on a psilocybin journey. I drank my psilocybin tea with five grams of mushrooms and cozied up in bed with my cat, inviting the wisdom of the fungi in. I set an intention to understand why this disease was in my body, how it related to my new path as a psychedelic psychotherapist, and how to best navigate whatever lay ahead.

Slowly, my mind slipped from my control, and images began to dance before me. Beautiful colors and patterns emerged, accompanied by a sense of calm mixed with an anxiousness that felt like urgency. I felt like I was on a subway speeding through the underground…or underworld. The doors would open at various stations, and I would disembark.

At one station, I was overwhelmed with fear. I saw and felt my mortality and experienced a profound sense of my body's impermanence, but this gave way to a calm and knowing that my energy and spirit were eternal and not dependent upon being in a body.

Suddenly, I was whisked to another station, where women I sensed were ancestors embraced me. Their kindness filled me with peace and calm. I sensed the generations as waves, ebbing and flowing across the shores of time. These women acknowledged my disease and let me know it had been carried energetically for many generations and that my healing would help heal us all, across space and time.

I was then whisked across time to another scene, and I could feel the presence of my mother, who had died from breast cancer. I received information about her cancer and my own, and was given insight to understand that our cancers were fear turned cellular. This resonated with me, as I was aware of fear-based internal dialogue and thought patterns that created anxiety. I knew this was not good for my emotional or physical health. I heard messages echoing, like wisdom from the mushrooms speaking…

You need to live joyfully.
Release the fear and live in trust.
Your life should be simple, soulful, and joyful.
Let these words guide your life and actions: simple, soulful, and joyful!

I then got a very clear vision and directive. It is hard to explain how these messages came through. For me, it was like knowledge was downloaded into my mind. The message I received was to go to the wilderness, find healing waters, and bathe my body to prepare for what was to come.

> The medicine speaks in symbols
> and sensation, in visions and in silence.
> Women know this language. It is the
> language of our ancestors and our souls.

As I slowly started to come out of my journey, I had a profound awareness that this experience was going to play a pivotal role in how I navigated my cancer. I also realized that by using this medicine on my cancer journey, I was gaining clarity on how to help others who had been diagnosed with cancer. Already I felt more empowered, and I had some clear areas of action to support my own healing by attending to my mind-body connection. My overwhelming fear had subsided, and I felt a deep sense of gratitude for the beauty and perfection of the way everything was unfolding and aligning in my life at this time. I had a sense that everything was happening as it was meant to, and that if I just released my fear to trust, I would be okay.

DISCOVERING MY PATH OF HEALING

Within weeks of my diagnosis, I had all the information I needed to make a medical treatment plan for my cancer. I decided to have a full double mastectomy, even though I only had a small spot of stage 1 DCIS (ductal carcinoma in situ) cancer in my left breast—a "speck" of cancer, as I referred to it. I had three weeks until the date of my surgery. I knew what I had to do.

A few days later, my husband and I hopped in our van and headed to the wilderness to find my healing water to prepare for the surgery ahead. We had no destination in mind, trusting that we would land wherever we were meant to be. Late that afternoon, we turned down a road to a remote campsite in Escalante, Utah. The camp host told us he had just one spot left, and it was perfect for our van. He mentioned a lovely hike through the canyon to a waterfall. I felt a tingle run through my whole body. There it was again, that deep sense of magic and that somehow there was so much more going on here than I could even begin to understand. As we began hiking down the gorgeous trail, the late-day sun warmed the ancient canyon walls that embraced us.

About an hour and a half into the canyon, the most amazing waterfall cascaded down from on high, filling a torquoise-blue pool at its base. There was no one anywhere to be seen. It felt like our own private wilderness. I stripped down, dove in, and bathed my body in the magical healing water as I had been guided to. A peace as powerful as any medicine filled my soul.

When I emerged from the pool, I dressed and began to walk barefoot along a small stream that led away from the pool at the base of the waterfall, feeling what can only be described as being in flow or floating outside of space and time. The bottom of the stream was pristine, soft, fine sand. Small fish swam around my feet, almost as if they were leading the way. They circled my legs then swam ahead…and then circled back to me, calling me on. I followed them—all faith, no fear.

I wandered down the stream for almost an hour, the little fish leading the way. And then, as if divinely guided, I emerged within a few feet of our van. The hours I spent that day in a state of total peace and trust and calm were powerful medicine emotionally, spiritually, and physiologically. Those states are known to boost and strengthen your immune system. As I fell asleep in the van that night, I was filled with excitement and a sense of purpose about turning my experience into an offering to help other women on their cancer journeys.

Two weeks later, I had my double mastectomy. I felt a great calm going through it, and I attribute this to my work with psilocybin.

My journey had given me a sense of empowerment. I knew the doctors could take care of the physical part of my cancer, but I now had a meaningful path to heal the mental, emotional, and spiritual aspect of my health as well. I had created a beautiful nature-based experience to prepare my body, mind, and spirit for the surgery. I gained new insights about outdated fear-based patterns of thought and created a practice to shift these patterns. I had assigned a sense of meaning to my disease that aligned with my personal belief system, helping me find peace and a path forward amidst a scary and seemingly random cancer diagnosis. My mushroom medicine was as important a part of my healing as modern Western medicine.

USING PSILOCYBIN TO REDUCE ILLNESS-RELATED ANXIETY

Research increasingly supports what many women have reported to me: Psilocybin can significantly reduce cancer-related anxiety and distress. Landmark clinical trials at Johns Hopkins[1] and New York University[2] found that a single moderate-to-high dose of psilocybin, given in a therapeutic setting, led to dramatic and sustained reductions in anxiety, depression, and existential fear in patients with life-threatening cancer diagnoses. In one study, up to 80% of participants experienced significant relief that persisted for six months or longer.[3] Many reported a shift in their relationship to death, describing a sense of deep peace, spiritual connection, or the feeling of being part of something larger than themselves.

Brain imaging studies suggest that psilocybin temporarily quiets the default mode network—the part of the brain involved in self-referential thinking and rumination—allowing for a break from fear-based mental loops. Together, these findings point to psilocybin not just as a psychological tool, but also as a spiritually informed intervention that helps you move from fear to acceptance, from anxiety to meaning.

I found all of these findings to be true for my own experience. My journey greatly reduced my fear as I navigated my cancer and gave me a path to integrate the experience to maintain that inner calm.

INTEGRATION PRACTICES FOR DISEASE AND CANCER

A disease diagnosis can create fear for your wellbeing, but it can also put you into a disconnected and conflicted relationship with your body. You may feel betrayed by it, angry with it, or dissociated from it.

Psychoneuroimmunology is the science of how emotional states impact your immune system. When dealing with a disease, self-care and compassion for your body become essential. Healing is amplified by hope and by positive emotional and psychological states.

So often women, who spend their lives caring for others, are unaware of their own needs. It's important to consider how you are framing this disease in your life and in your body. Explore the ways you can feel empowered to support your own healing, even if that is just staying positive. Give your body love and compassion.

Here are a few self-care techniques that can support your mind-body connection while you are healing or navigating a health challenge. These activities can help you feel empowered and connected to your body and assist you in accessing the power of the mind-body connection to promote healing.

- **Healing Ritual Bath:** Create a ritual bath with herbs, intention, and music. Imagine this is healing water. What do you need the water to heal? It can be physical, emotional, or spiritual. Light a candle and play a lovely soundscape like a river, waves, or rain to help you envision you are healing in a magical place in the wilderness.

- **Guided Meditation:** Journey inward to meet your inner-healing wisdom and ask your body what it needs from you. See the Dear Reader page at the end of the book for a link to a guided meditation to put you in a state of deep relaxation and help you connect to the wisdom within that is there to support your healing intelligence.

- **Affirmation:** Think of your body as your partner in life, who you travel this experience of living with. How do you talk to and treat your body? Create a few affirmation statements like the ones below that send your body love.

"My body is strong and beautiful."
"My body knows how to heal."
"Thank you, sweet body, for all you do to support me and help me enjoy this life."

Journaling Prompts

1. Write about a time you experienced a significant illness or disease. What narrative did you create to accompany that experience?

2. Did you see yourself as a victim, a warrior, a healer? Perhaps a bit of all three?

3. What lessons did you learn from that experience?

4. What is your relationship like with your body from the experience of illness or disease?

CHAPTER 2

A Lick of Healing

> You don't have to control your thoughts; you just have to stop letting them control you.
>
> — DAN MILLMAN

I tell all my clients who have severe anxiety that it's like having a really mean bully living in your head. That bully is actually your amygdala sending out warning messages and trying to keep you safe, but these excessive warnings become the problem. The task is to rewire your brain and that voice and build a sense of safety. Psilocybin has a wonderful way of calming and rewiring your inner alarm system.

If you suffer from obsessive-compulsive disorder (OCD), you know all about the intrusive thoughts and the anxiety-driven rituals or mental compulsions that disrupt your emotional wellbeing. It can often lead to chronic stress, shame, and feelings of isolation. In women, it is also frequently exacerbated by hormonal shifts, life transitions, and trauma histories, making it especially challenging to manage without integrated, trauma-informed support. OCD affects millions of people worldwide. Research suggests that approximately 1 in 100 women will experience OCD at some point in their lives.[4] While it is often associated with overt compulsions like handwashing or checking, many women struggle with more internalized symptoms—such as obsessive thoughts and rumination about dangers, contamination, or relationships—that can go unnoticed and undiagnosed for years.[5]

RENEE'S JOURNEY

Renee was a beautiful woman in her forties. She had a rich, full life in a desirable suburb of Seattle. She, her husband, and her 12-year-old son loved to travel, hike, and foster dogs in need. All of this changed when the pandemic hit. Renee contracted COVID and went to the hospital, where she then got a very bad intestinal infection. She was sick for months and became increasingly fearful of germs and contamination. Her obsessive fear made it hard for her to leave the house.

She had been working with a therapist doing EMDR (eye movement desensitization and reprocessing) and exposure therapy for over a year. Although it helped a little, she felt that overall she was getting worse. Eager to help her, Renee's husband started researching new and alternative treatments for OCD, which led him to an article on the use of psilocybin-assisted therapy. He shared it with Renee, who was intrigued, and in turn, she shared it with her psychiatrist. Her doctor had been following the growing field of psychedelic therapy and felt this might be a promising treatment for Renee, if done with a therapist skilled in OCD. With a little research, they came across my work as a certified anxiety disorder treatment specialist working with all manner of anxiety disorders and with psilocybin.

After weeks of phone and email discussion, I met with Renee for the first time in my office. It was no small feat for her to board a plane and travel to see me. Despite the stress that travel caused her, she wore a warm, open smile, but her anxiety showed in her inability to touch doorknobs without a tissue protecting her hand.

I was excited that Renee found me, because I felt confident that a journey would be a step forward in helping to decrease her OCD. She was eager to have enough relief from her symptoms so she could return to the things in life that brought her joy, like fostering dogs and kissing her husband. These two activities, she told me tearfully, were currently too triggering for her. I was filled with compassion for her and committed to supporting her in reaching for those beautiful and significant goals.

Renee came to me with a good mindset for a journey. She was eager and ready to reclaim her brain and inner peace. At its core, anxiety is your brain's threat-detection system misfiring. Your brain is wired for survival, constantly scanning for danger and activating the fight-or-flight response when it perceives a threat. This system is essential when real danger is present, but in anxiety, the brain falsely interprets harmless situations as threats, triggering the same physiological response—racing heart, rapid breathing, muscle tension, and heightened alertness. Renee's misfiring amygdala—the part of the brain responsible for processing fear—thought it was helping her stay safe, but it had now in fact become the problem.

The neuroplastic state that the psilocybin creates would give her the opportunity to rewire and correct this pattern in her mind.

On journey day, Renee was as excited as she was nervous. But she had a deep sense of trust in the process and in her own inner-healing intelligence. We had spent several weeks getting to know each other over the phone, so she also felt very safe and comfortable with me. We agreed the journey would take place at an old farmhouse she had rented for the weekend. It was a beautiful spot in the country, and the peacefulness would certainly enhance her experience. She brought her own favorite mug for the medicine tea, one that her son had made for her in pottery class. We brewed her mushrooms into a tea with lemon, ginger, and honey. She sipped thoughtfully, whispering her intentions, as she settled into the music and began to journey.

About an hour after she finished her tea, she called me over and said she wanted a lemon drop candy from her bedside table. I opened it carefully and gave it to her directly from the wrapper. This was the only way she could put anything in her mouth. Because of the OCD, her food could never be touched by any human hands. She took the lemon drop from the wrapper and into her mouth and sucked on it for a few minutes. Then she abruptly took my hand and spit the candy into my palm.

"That isn't working for me" she said, taking a sip of water.

Less than a minute later, she took my hand and licked the candy off my palm and into her mouth.

I paused, expecting her to be triggered and freak out, but she rolled over and journeyed quietly for the next hour.

A Lick of Healing

Exposure therapy is the tried-and-true technique of gradually exposing someone to their OCD trigger so they build up a tolerance and become less reactive to it. And here, in this highly neuroplastic and psychologically flexible state, Renee's brain was literally seeking the stimulus so it could respond differently and thus create new neural pathways around her germ triggers. A bit later, she asked for another lemon drop and again ate it right from my fingers! I had not planned or orchestrated this. This was her own inner-healing intelligence at work doing exactly what was needed to rewire her anxious OCD brain.

> Psilocybin opens the door, but it is the woman's soul that walks through it. Her healing is not in the substance, but in her courage to face what lies within.

Later that afternoon when she emerged from her journey, one of the first things she asked me was "Did I lick your hand?"

I told her that she did indeed eat candy out of my hand a couple of times...and even licked my palm once.

Her reaction was surprisingly calm.

"That is so crazy, I can't believe I did that," she said.
"Does thinking about that make you feel anxious?"
"No, not at all, which is so weird," she replied.

Weird indeed—and powerful. This psilocybin-supported exposure-therapy session retrained her brain in the most effective of ways.

She told me about another part of her journey where she had a conversation with the mushrooms, who told her that her gut biome and body are host to lots of different bacteria and that most of them are good and necessary for her health. The mushrooms encouraged her to think of bacteria as allies, not enemies. This was a powerful perspective shift that she knew would help her move forward. As part of her integration, I encouraged her to turn that statement into an affirmation card she could post as a reminder: BACTERIA ARE MY ALLIES, NOT ENEMIES!

She shared how her journey had brought her back though time, where she saw all sorts of symbols she didn't recognize but somehow knew were from very early forms of religion. It made her feel a strong calling to connect with her own sense of spirituality. She had a deep understanding that her obsession with germs had been a distraction keeping her from connecting with herself and her daily life, but that it was also preventing her from connecting with the divine. When she returned home, she wanted to explore world religions and the symbols she had seen on her journey.

As we processed the experience, she sketched some of the symbols she had seen and was excited to determine whether they too had messages that might relate to her healing path. She felt a new excitement about seeing herself and the world through more of a spiritual journey lens and felt that even the OCD was somehow part of stirring this awakening. When she flew out a day later, she called from the airport to say she still was not feeling triggered by germs, not even in the crowded airport while touching all those surfaces. This was a dramatic shift and represented so much healing.

On our six-month follow-up call, Renee shared that while she still was more hypervigilant than most people about germs and cleanliness, she was once again able to foster dogs and make out with her husband. Her ability to engage in activities that brought her joy and to have a greater sense of mastery over her anxiety were the true measure of success. I used many classic therapy modalities as part of her integration, but I have no doubt that the neuroplastic state and rewiring session on psilocybin had the greatest impact on her outcome.

PSILOCYBIN AND OCD

I was so intrigued by the spontaneous exposure-therapy experience that Renee had on psilocybin that I connected with a researcher at London Imperial College, Sorcha O'Connor. Sorcha's PsilOCD study involved a small study group on low-dose psilocybin exploring its effects on OCD.[6] Her ongoing research hopes to illuminate the clinical effectiveness of such interventions. In her small sample so far, she has seen positive outcomes and decreases in patients' levels of anxiety and obsessive behaviors. She was fascinated by the client experience I shared with her and hoped the UK would one day be able to offer such services outside of the very limited clinical research studies currently available.

While we can explain part of Renee's experience as brain rewiring via exposure therapy in a neuroplastic state, we cannot explain how or why she spontaneously engaged in this activity as her mushrooms kicked in. To me, that is a perfect example of the inner-healing intelligence.

Emerging research is showing significant promise for the use of psilocybin-assisted therapy in treating OCD. A landmark 2006 study at the University of Arizona found that a single dose of psilocybin led to acute and sometimes sustained reductions in OCD symptoms in participants.[7] More recent trials, including those at Yale and Johns Hopkins, are exploring the potential of psilocybin to interrupt the rigid neural loops associated with OCD by promoting neural plasticity and increasing connectivity between brain regions.[8]

In my own work with clients, I have seen women experience some reprieve from obsessive thought patterns and gain new perspectives on their inner experience. Combining skilled therapeutic support with psilocybin therapy can offer a new healing path for women living with OCD.

INTEGRATION PRACTICES FOR OCD

In the days and weeks after my clients' journeys, I guide them to gently challenge compulsions and obsessive thinking through exposure and response prevention (ERP) techniques—now made more effective by the brain's increased openness to change. This is an ideal window for cognitive restructuring, where clients can begin practicing new behaviors, engaging with feared stimuli without ritualizing, and cultivating self-compassion. Mindfulness-based strategies, journaling, and parts work can support women in their effort to observe obsessive patterns without identifying with them, while somatic and breath-based practices anchor the nervous system. Integration during this sensitive period is about reinforcing insight gained during the journey and actively supporting the brain in forming new, more adaptive neural circuitry aligned with freedom, agency, and emotional resilience.

While I have spoken of OCD in this chapter, anxiety can take many forms. The activities below can be helpful for any level of anxiety and might help you regain more control over that bully voice.

- **Try the Parts Work Exercise.** Talk with your inner protector part, the part that warns you constantly about all the possible dangers, real and imagined, in an effort to keep you safe. This is also what makes you shrink back from life due to fear. This part thinks it is protecting you, but it has become the problem.

  1. Ask some questions and get to know it better.
     - When did you first show up in my life? (Think about when this voice started guiding your behavior.)
     - What are you trying to protect me from?
     - How can you help me feel safe in a different way?
  2. Give this part a name.
  3. Imagine how it looks and sounds. It can be helpful to understand that it is not trying to be a problem; it really thinks it is helping you.
  4. Bring some compassion to it as you help it find a new job and let it know you are safe.

The book *Taming Your Gremlin: A Surprisingly Simple Method for Getting Out of Your Own Way* by Rick Carson offers some fun strategies for this technique.

- **Teach your body and brain to feel safe.** Spend 10 minutes three times a day—morning, noon, and night—in a quiet state of calm. You don't need to learn a complicated form of meditation. Simply bring your attention to your breath and the present moment.

1. Find a quiet place to sit, either in nature or looking at a picture of nature.

2. Notice how your body feels supported by whatever you are sitting on.

3. Notice any sounds you hear.

4. Envision your breath like waves rolling in and out.

5. Maintain an awareness of your breath, of the sounds around you, and of your body being supported. Let your thoughts float past.

6. Spend 10 minutes just being, not doing.

This simple activity of being present supports your nervous system and helps you learn how it feels to be in a calm and relaxed body. It trains your brain to recognize a path to calm and how to be in a relaxed state. To make it even more powerful, find an aromatherapy oil that you use only when you are doing relaxation breathing. Choose a scent like fresh oranges, rosemary, or lavender—one that reminds you of a happy memory. Link that scent to your relaxation, and it will become a trigger to help your brain call up the relaxation response.

Journaling Prompts

These prompts will help you reflect on your inner freedom and imagine a life beyond compulsive behavior, anchoring insights from the psilocybin journey into concrete emotional visioning.

1. When do I feel the most calm and relaxed?
2. What or who is that relaxed part of me? How can I invite that part to be more present in my life?
3. If my inner fear voice were gone, what would I do less or more of?

CHAPTER 3

Rising from the Ashes

> The doors to the world of the wild Self are few but precious. If you have a deep scar, that is a door. If you have an old, old story, that is a door. If you love the sky and the water so much you almost cannot bear it, that is a door. If you yearn for a deeper life, a full life, a sane life, that is a door.
>
> — CLARISSA PINKOLA ESTÉS

Women are healers, helpers, nurturers, and caregivers. Often, in giving, we can lose parts of ourselves and accept behaviors that are not in our own best interests. Maybe that is why post-traumatic stress disorder (PTSD) affects women at nearly twice the rate of men, with studies indicating that women face a two-to-threefold increased risk of PTSD and demonstrate a lifetime prevalence of between 10% and 12% for women and between 5% and 6% for men.[9] Many women experience trauma through relationship violence, childhood neglect, or workplace abuse—often compounded by the societal pressure to suppress or minimize their suffering.

PTSD can profoundly impact your emotional wellbeing, leading to chronic anxiety, hypervigilance, intrusive memories, nightmares, emotional numbness, or difficulty trusting others. These symptoms can disrupt your relationships, lower your self-esteem, and reduce the ability to feel safe in your own body, often leaving you feeling disconnected from your inner resilience and sense of self.

MEGAN'S JOURNEY

Megan came to one of my retreats and found healing for PTSD she wasn't even aware she was harboring. She had agreed to come at the prodding of her best friend of 20 years, Shannon. For the previous two years, Shannon had been reading about psychedelic therapy and watching many documentaries. She was fascinated and really wanted to do a retreat but didn't want to go alone. For months, she had been sharing all the research and talking Megan's ear off about psilocybin retreats. Finally, Megan agreed—under the condition that it be a woman-only retreat led by a mature and skilled facilitator. Our retreats fit that bill.

When I met with Megan on our first discovery call to screen her for the retreat, she indicated that her intention was to explore her consciousness and enhance her personal development. She didn't mention any past trauma, though she shared that she had done therapy on and off over the years for normal stressors such as relationship issues.

Megan was retired after a two-decade career as a firefighter. She was proud of her ability to hold her own in this male-dominated field. Although it was a stressful career with its share of challenges, she felt she had processed all that and was now eager to explore herself a bit more deeply as she entered retirement.

Megan's retreat took place on an absolutely beautiful fall weekend at a mountain inn tucked into the woods near a crystal-clear creek. Shannon and Megan were sharing a two-bedroom cabin. The other guests were scattered about the property in other cabins. My retreat partner Monica and I shared the big cabin, where we held all the gatherings and activities in a great room. The setting couldn't have been more ideally suited for our purposes.

In our opening circle on the first evening of the retreat, Megan introduced herself and told us her intention for coming on the retreat was to support her friend and explore her own consciousness. She said she had spent part of her career working as a firefighter, which she found rewarding but at times challenging and stressful. Her squad had a therapist who had helped her process some of the more traumatic calls she had responded to over the years. She felt she had handled past traumas well and was confident she would have a good journey, focused on her future.

I reminded her, as I always do, that one never knew what they would encounter—but whatever arose was there to serve in her healing.

"What meets you is meant for you" and "Be curious, not fearful" are my go-to mottos in preparing people for a journey.

Given Megan's history, I wondered whether some challenging material might arise, so I tried to temper her expectations. This is always a tricky dance, however, as you never know what type of journey someone will have. And as much as you want them to be ready for some shadow work, you also want to be careful not to plant any fearful thoughts. The other helpful prep reminder I share with everyone is that their journey will have a beginning, a middle, and an end. Within five to six hours, they will be back. And no one ever gets lost.

The next morning, Megan and Shannon were both excited yet nervous, which is common on journey day. During a morning ceremony, the women stated their intentions and then participated in a guided meditation. After they drank their tea, Megan and Shannon returned to their cabin with a schoolgirl-like giddiness. They did a big hug and wished each other a happy journey before going to their respective rooms and settling into their beds. I reminded them that I would be attuned and attentive and checking in all day, holding space and support for them both.

During Megan's journey, she lay in her bed behind her eye mask with a very intense and serious look on her face. She barely moved at all for two hours, but then she began to cry loudly, her body heaving with grief. She pulled handfuls of tissue from the box on her bed and could barely keep up with the tears that drenched her face. Her floor was littered with scrunched bunches of tear-soaked Kleenex. She cried for hours and then appeared to fall asleep.

Meanwhile, Shannon had begun giggling quietly in her room, a wide smile across her face. At hour five, she sat up and said she was back and wanted to go sit by the stream with her journal. She tiptoed past Megan's room and saw her floor littered with a sea of tissues. I assured her that her friend was fine, and she continued out to the stream.

When Megan came out of her journey about a half hour later, she said she had a pounding headache from hours of crying and moving through intense emotion. I got her water with electrolytes and sat with her. She said the journey had been much harder and more physical than she expected. She wasn't ready to talk about it but added that it had been both difficult and powerful and that despite the headache, she felt a certain lightness, like she had let a lot of stuff go. She didn't want to go outside or talk with anyone just yet and asked to have her dinner brought to her room. I brought her a warm bowl of soup and baguette, the perfect comfort food after a long day's journey. She savored her meal, showered, and went to bed early that night.

Saturday morning, the six women assembled in a circle in our great room. Some chatted cheerfully as they arrived, while others were quiet and reflective. As they settled in, Monica chimed the bell and invited the group to close their eyes, focus their breath, and ground themselves in the space and present moment. I lit a candle and made a few statements about the process for our integration circle. Each person would get about 20 minutes to share their experience, and Monica and I would offer guidance and support to each person to help them understand the mystical experience and powerful psycho-spiritual journey from the day before. We explained that we would help them tease out the key insights and strategize how to use and integrate them to change and heal old patterns of thought and outdated beliefs.

It was during this process of integration that they would harvest the rich gifts from their inner wisdom. Sometimes the insights didn't come right away but instead settled over them like the warm sun.

Often the guests who had the most joyful journeys were eager to go first in our sharing circle. For this reason, I started by speaking about how every person had a very different and unique experience that was right for them. I spoke of the importance of being respectful of each other's stories and holding compassionate attention to each other's sharings, recognizing that some might have struggled with hard journeys and others may have had happy ones. There are no right or wrong journeys; they are different and unique to each person.

With ground rules laid, we began. When Megan raised her hand to share, I had no idea what her journey had been, as she had yet to speak of it to anyone, even Shannon. She asked for the tissue box, took a deep breath, and began. She said as the medicine came on, she felt waves of fear. The feeling of letting go was terrifying and gripped her for the first hour. But she remembered my words "Be curious, not fearful" and eventually was able to release control and become an observer of her experience. She felt a heavy weight on her, like her clothes weighed hundreds of pounds. She understood this as some sort of protection she had carried for years. It was a substantial sadness and she felt like she had cried years' worth of tears.

Then at some point, she had been overcome with an insight that this protection she wore wasn't keeping the hard emotions of sadness and grief out; it was locking those feelings in. She remembered pulling off her covers, which symbolized opening up to let all that grief and sadness and armor go. She recalled at one point walking into a house where she had put a raging fire out years ago.

She entered the master bedroom of the burned home, and on the bed were a man and woman in an embrace. They were beautiful, young, and healthy. They sat up and looked straight at her from their scorched room.

"Why are you still thinking about us?" they asked. "We have moved on and never think about you!"

As she told the circle about this part of her journey, she shared that many years ago she had entered a home after a fire and found a couple in an embrace, burned and deceased. She thought she had dealt with that trauma but said that their appearance in her journey had released her from that traumatic memory in a beautiful and meaningful way that made her feel lighter. She felt like she had let that couple and that scary memory go. She said the journey had been hard on her emotionally and physically, but she would do it again in a heartbeat for the healing and release she received.

For the rest of the weekend, I could see and feel the shift in Megan's energy. She laughed more and carried herself in a way that seemed lighter. As part of her integration plan, I gave her a journaling prompt to explore all the events and encounters she may have had in the past that she was still carrying but could now release.

I shared with her the Zen parable about the monk and his assistant who encountered a very rude woman on a trail. She insisted they carry her and her belongings across a muddy patch and then dismissed them rudely. A few hours later, the young monk asked the older monk why he had helped the rude woman.

The older monk replied calmly, "I put that woman down hours ago. Why are *you* still carrying her?"

I encouraged Megan to get index cards and write goodbye notes to any memories that she now recognized were not serving her and she could release. I instructed her to take each card and burn it, imagining it leaving her as it fell into ashes. There is a power in such rituals of release. I also encouraged her to create a mantra, affirmation, or motto to help her welcome her new perspective on embracing grief. Although she didn't fancy herself an artist, she thought she might find a way to capture that as an image she could create to remind her. Because so much of the wisdom we receive in medicine work comes through in images, symbols, and metaphors, art can be a fabulous tool for integration.

Megan came to our retreat seeking one thing and left receiving something that her heart really needed. Her inner-healing intelligence guided her journey and spoke to her in a language that her soul understood.

USING PSILOCYBIN TO OVERCOME PTSD

Recent research into psilocybin-assisted therapy is offering hope for those suffering from PTSD. Emerging neuroimaging studies suggest that psilocybin can calm activity in the amygdala. In healthy volunteers, a single acute dose significantly reduced amygdala reactivity to negative or neutral stimuli, and these decreases correlated with increases in positive mood states.[10] Studies suggest,[11] and my own experience has shown, that psilocybin may help women access and process traumatic memories from a more compassionate, non-defensive state of awareness. In combination with supportive therapy, this can allow for the release of deeply held fear and shame, and the integration of trauma in a way that fosters healing rather than retraumatization. Early-phase clinical trials and anecdotal reports are showing that even a single guided psilocybin session can bring significant and lasting relief from PTSD symptoms, making it a promising frontier in trauma therapy.[12]

When you connect with this deep inner-healing intelligence, you are in essence healing yourself. It is a beautiful and empowering process to trust yourself and the wisdom within.

INTEGRATION PRACTICES FOR DEALING WITH TRAUMA AND POST-TRAUMATIC STRESS DISORDER

Integration therapy for clients who have used psilocybin to treat PTSD focuses on translating the insights and emotional breakthroughs of the journey into lasting neural and behavioral change. With the heightened neuroplasticity comes the opportunity to rewire and reinforce neural pathways and brain patterns that tell a new story about resilience and personal power.

Internal Family Systems (IFS) is a therapeutic model that was developed by Dr. Richard "Dick" Schwartz in the 1980s.[13] It conceptualizes the mind as made up of multiple parts, each with its own perspectives, emotions, and roles. Trauma often creates exiled parts, which hold painful memories and emotions, and protective parts that attempt to manage or suppress the pain. IFS helps individuals access their core self—a calm, compassionate, and curious center—to safely interact with these parts, promote healing, and restore internal harmony. IFS allows for deeper healing and integration of insights gained during a psychedelic experience, supporting lasting emotional transformation and personal empowerment.

- **Talk to your wounded self.** In this exercise, you meet and dialogue with a wounded part of yourself that surfaced during your psilocybin experience. Ask your injured self these questions:
    - "What do you need me to know about what you felt and experienced?"
    - "What would help you feel safe now?"
    - "Is there a protector part that shows up when you feel threatened?"

    This builds connection between your adult self and vulnerable inner parts, supporting trauma resolution from the inside out.

- **Do a vagus nerve reset with touch and breath.** This supports regulation and interrupts trauma-driven hypervigilance, reinforcing safety in the body.
    1. Place one hand over your heart, the other on your belly.
    2. Breathe slowly into your belly (inhale for 4 counts, exhale for 6).
    3. After several rounds, introduce a gentle rocking motion or hum to stimulate the vagus nerve.

Journaling Prompts

1. What part of me needed to survive, and what part of me is now ready to feel safe and live fully?

   This prompt helps you honor the protective adaptations you've made in response to trauma while inviting deeper self-compassion and readiness to grow beyond them.

2. When do I feel the most safe and comfortable in my body? How can I turn this into a relaxation ritual to help train my mind-body connection to have a consistent path to relaxation?

3. I feel safe when...

4. Write an exhaustive list of all the things that make you feel safe.

CHAPTER 4

Inviting Your Inner Child Home

> Healing your lost inner-child wounding takes time, gentle care, and learning to love and embrace your wounded parts.
>
> — ROBERT JACKMAN

Why is it so hard for us as women to nurture ourselves, even though we can be so good at taking care of others? Often we learn from an early age to keep our needs quiet—not to help us, but to accommodate others. Many of the women I have worked with carry wounded inner-child parts as a result of unmet emotional needs, childhood neglect, abuse, or experiences of feeling unseen, unheard, or unsafe during formative years.

If you are carrying wounded parts, they may be operating below your conscious awareness. But they can profoundly impact your emotional wellbeing, leading to patterns of self-criticism, people-pleasing, emotional reactivity, fear of abandonment, or difficulty trusting others. Your inner child may manifest as anxiety, perfectionism, chronic shame, or an aching sense of not being "enough." Left unaddressed, these unresolved wounds from your early years can create inner conflict and block your access to joy, creativity, and self-compassion.

In Cathy's case, a childhood filled with abuse and isolation had built her into a wounded warrior with a lost inner child she needed to bring home.

CATHY'S JOURNEY

Cathy, a strong and tall woman with a kind face, exuded confidence when she came to me. But as our conversation unfolded, she revealed that she had struggled with a lifetime of PTSD from her abusive childhood. Her single mother had worked nights most of Cathy's childhood. These circumstances often left Cathy with inappropriate caregivers, many of whom became her abusers.

Her uncle sometimes stayed at the house and invited friends over for bouts of heavy drinking. She experienced sexual abuse from about age 7 to 16, when she left home. She spent much of her childhood running off across the field by her house and hiding in the woods.

There was a calm matter-of-factness to the way Cathy shared these experiences, because she had built strong armor to protect and disconnect herself from the deep pain associated with them.

Cathy had heard from her therapist that psilocybin was proving helpful for people suffering from PTSD. After doing her own research, she was intrigued by the healing that veterans were experiencing. She felt that her childhood trauma was akin to having served in battle in many ways.

As she was scouting the internet on the topic of psilocybin, she came across a CBS special that Lisa Ling had done on a retreat I had run. Cathy felt like this was not a coincidence but a sign for us to connect. I received her email, and we spoke over Zoom a week later. I was struck by Cathy's openness and desire to heal. She had done much work already with her therapist and had realistic expectations for psilocybin to support and enhance the work she was already doing. Her intention was to find a way to connect with and heal her inner child. She sensed that part of her healing work needed to happen at deeper levels than those she could access through talk therapy.

The day of her journey, the sky was bright blue and clear. Snow still clung to the mountain peaks visible through the window of the office. A ray of warm sunlight heated up the comfy couch where she would be journeying for the day. She was nervous but determined. We had discussed how to use breathing techniques if any anxiety arose, and she knew I would be there to support her as needed. Cathy placed a picture of herself as a little girl on the table beside her next to a large tissue box. We dimmed the lights, then she sipped her mushroom tea, lay back, pulled up her blanket, donned her headphones, and drifted off on her inner journey.

As Cathy slipped into a state of non-ordinary consciousness, she saw her little self at about age nine. She was a fierce little tomboy wearing a self-fashioned loincloth tied around her waist with a little bow and arrow flung across her back. Cathy remembered that outfit and could almost feel how it had felt on her little nine-year-old body. She was witnessing herself at this age, but was also simultaneously being herself at nine. She was flooded with memories and emotions. She remembered how much she had loved pretending she was a warrior fighting off all the imaginary enemies that inhabited her world in the woods. No one could hurt her there. She was strong and brave. Her bow and arrow gave her almost magical strength and ferocity.

But the adult Cathy, whose consciousness was also present as an observer in this journey, knew this Little Cathy had no choice but to pretend to be brave, even though she was scared and a victim of the enemies she could not escape. Cathy's heart welled with empathy for her child self. A wave of self-compassion washed over her. She watched Little Cathy run off and hide in the woods. She called after her but couldn't find her. Her heart ached, and she felt a powerful pull to hug, hold, and comfort her little wounded warrior self.

> Healing begins the moment you turn toward the tender forgotten parts of yourself with love.

When you hold your inner child with compassion, you remember that you were never broken—just waiting to be seen, soothed, and safely loved back into wholeness.

Her journey continued to take many twists and turns as she traveled across various times, ages, stages, people, and relationships in her life. Each section of her journey revealed the circumstances that had shaped her strength, confidence, and personal power. She was shown her resilience in all its glory and was able to feel a deep love and gratitude to herself that she hadn't felt before. She felt whole, not broken...victorious, not victimized. For the first time in her life, she had a sense of self-worth. She emerged from her journey elated. Never before had she felt these emotions of self-love and self-acceptance. She cried for almost an hour as she spoke of feeling freed from the shame and self-loathing that had followed her almost all her life.

As she described her little warrior self with bow and arrow, she said, "I was such an awesome little badass! I wish I could show my little self what an awesome big badass we have grown up to be."

My reply startled her. "You *can* show her, and you absolutely *should* show her. As a matter of fact, I think you should go back there and invite her to come live with you!"

I asked Cathy if she wanted me to lead her on a guided meditation to go find Little Cathy.

"Absolutely!" was her reply.

She leaned back, and I led her through a few breaths. I then invited her to see the field that Little Cathy had run across and the woods just beyond where she had gone to hide. I told her to go find Little Cathy and invite her to leave the past and come live safely here and now with her grown-up self. Cathy lay quietly in the meditation for about 15 minutes. From my seat at the bedside,

I watched a wide smile spread across her face as she rolled over and hugged her pillow.

She opened her eyes and in almost a whisper said, "I've got her. She is safely here with me now and forever. I have brought her home."

With tears welling, I walked quietly out of the room to let Cathy have some privacy. She would later tell me that in the guided meditation, she had driven into that field in her big pick-up truck that she drove in real life, and she called Little Cathy, who had peeked out from the bushes. "Come on, hop in. You can leave this place forever to come live with me!"

Little Cathy ran out from the bushes and hopped up into the front seat of the truck next to Big Cathy. "This is a fierce, badass truck," she said, laying her bow and arrow down on the seat next to her.

Big Cathy said, "Yes it is, and so am I. And no one will ever hurt you again."

Cathy's medicine journey, followed by her guided imagery meditation, gave her a real and powerful way to heal and connect with her wounded inner child. Her journey was more powerful for healing her PTSD than all the years of talk therapy she had engaged in. This experience was an opportunity to time-travel and rescue her wounded child from the past.

As part of her ongoing integration, I encouraged Cathy to deepen her relationship with Little Cathy by doing inner-child guided meditations where she would imagine spending time with her younger self. Two months after her journey, when we did our final integration, the way she spoke of Little Cathy revealed how very real and present she now was in her life. She had reparented this lost part of herself and helped her develop the self-compassion and self-love she found on her journey. Cathy even got a little kid's bow and arrow set, which she put on her wall as a reminder of the brave little badass she was and how that had helped her grow into the beautiful bold badass she is today. This healing was such a beautiful representation of how critical it is to keep an open heart to welcome our wounded inner-child parts home.

USING PSILOCYBIN TO ADDRESS INNER-CHILD ISSUES

Psilocybin therapy is emerging as a promising approach for addressing childhood trauma, often conceptualized as "inner-child wounds." Research indicates that psychedelics like psilocybin can facilitate profound emotional processing and healing by enhancing neuroplasticity and reducing hyperactivity in trauma-related brain regions.

One study found that individuals with a history of adverse childhood experiences who had used psilocybin reported lower levels of psychological distress compared to those who had not, suggesting potential benefits in treating the psychological consequences of such experiences.[14]

Psilocybin's ability to reduce amygdala reactivity may help diminish the emotional intensity of trauma recall, facilitating a more compassionate and integrated processing of past wounds.

Under the influence of psilocybin, the brain shifts into a more flexible, interconnected state, allowing deep emotional memories and symbolic experiences to emerge. In this expanded state of consciousness, many individuals encounter their younger selves with surprising clarity, often feeling waves of compassion, forgiveness, and understanding toward parts of themselves that had long been buried or suppressed. This therapy creates an opportunity to time-travel back to our inner children and have powerful and meaningful interactions with our little selves. Therapists such as myself who are trained on IFS and other parts-based approaches are finding that psilocybin journeys can greatly accelerate the healing process by making these inner-child parts feel seen, loved, and safely integrated into the adult self. This integration can lead to profound shifts in emotional regulation, self-worth, and a renewed sense of wholeness.

Early in my career as a therapist, I thought it was a distraction to have clients spend sessions going back in time to revisit traumatic experiences from their childhoods. I thought it was more important to focus on attending to the here and now and developing skills and strategies to self-regulate, set boundaries, and amplify resilience.

Over the years, I have come to learn that every one of us has inner-child parts that desperately need our love and attention. Whether you had a beautiful childhood or a challenging one, that little girl within still wants you to know her, love her, and understand her—and in doing so, you bring a greater richness and capacity for joy to your adult self.

The way clients connect with, and encounter, their inner child when on psilocybin is often very profound and life-changing. It can also be surprising to discover the wounds that inner child carries. Sometimes she needs help releasing an incident that you dismissed as insignificant at the time. Conversely, your inner child can remind you of the wisdom you carry, or she might invite you to reconnect to parts of yourself that you lost along the way. Either way, building a relationship with your inner child reaps beautiful rewards.

INTEGRATION PRACTICES THAT SUPPORT INNER-CHILD HEALING

Integration therapy for clients who have used psilocybin to heal inner-child wounds focuses on nurturing and reparenting the vulnerable, exiled parts of the self that often carry shame, fear, or unmet needs from early life experiences. Psilocybin journeys frequently open a deep emotional connection to these wounded child parts—offering clarity, compassion, and insight into their origin stories.

In the neuroplastic weeks following the journey, the brain is especially open to forming new relational patterns and beliefs, making it an ideal time to introduce inner-child healing rituals, parts dialogue, and somatic safety practices. This is the time I help clients replace old self-critical or abandonment-based patterns with new ones rooted in self-trust, emotional validation, and compassionate self-leadership. Think of it like traveling back in time to help your younger self with the wisdom you have now as your older self.

- **Daily Inner-Child Check-In:** Set aside five minutes each morning to connect with the child part that emerged in the journey. Ask her: "How are you feeling today? What do you need from me?" and offer a visualized act of comfort, such as a hug or a reassuring word.

- **Protector Dialogue:** Invite the part of you that usually takes over (perfectionist, controller, avoider) to speak. Ask her: "What are you trying to protect me from? Would you be open to letting the adult self lead today?"

- **Inner-Child Letter Writing:** Write a letter to your inner child from your adult self, offering reassurance. Then write a letter *from* your inner child to your adult self, expressing feelings, needs, or gratitude post-journey.

- **Embodied Reparenting Practice:** While lying down or seated with eyes closed, imagine holding your inner child. Breathe slowly and repeat affirmations such as…

  - "You are safe now."
  - "I've got you."
  - "You matter."

This activates neural safety pathways and reinforces new self-relating patterns.

Journaling Prompts

1. What did my inner child most need to hear, feel, or receive that they didn't before?

2. How can I show up for this part of me now, in a way no one else could then?

3. How can I play with my inner child? What activity could I do that would just be about having fun?

CHAPTER 5

Breaking Chains

> In the stillness of the journey, she met the voice she had silenced for years. It was not the medicine that healed her—it was the reunion with her own truth.
>
> — UNKNOWN

Society teaches us to honor our commitments, and as women we often do so at the expense of our own wellbeing. Unfortunately, way too many women find themselves in narcissistic abusive relationships.[15] Psilocybin journeys reveal these patterns like a mirror to the soul. Even if you are a strong, confident woman, you can fall prey to this type of relationship abuse.

Subtle manipulation, gaslighting, and emotional control can erode your sense of reality and self-worth over time. This form of abuse can have profound and lasting impacts on your emotional wellbeing, resulting in chronic anxiety, depression, self-doubt, shame, and/or a deep disconnection from your inner truth and power. The invisible wounds of narcissistic abuse can leave you feeling isolated, confused, and emotionally depleted.

ROSE'S JOURNEY

Like several other women I have helped recover from this abuse, Rose was outwardly strong and self-confident—but inside, she was beaten down and in need of healing.

As Rose entered the circle on a warm afternoon in Mexico, she looked nervous. As the guests arrived, they all took seats under a large awning, the jungle off to one side and ocean beckoning beyond. These guests had journeyed from all over the world—not for the tropical ambiance, but to heal wounds they carried in their minds and emotions. It was a circle of seekers, eager to ease their pain. It was an eclectic group in age, economics, and appearances—from shabby to chic. An outsider looking in at this group would never in a million years be able to guess that what had brought them together was the call to try psilocybin medicine.

Rose was a well-dressed woman in her late fifties who carried herself in a way that suggested a life spent in comfortable surrounds. While other guests made small talk as they waited for the group to begin, she sat quietly, self-contained.

As the meeting opened and the introductions began, I could feel everyone's nervous but excited energy. All of these guests had taken a huge leap of faith in coming to this island to take a psychedelic journey that would allow them to reclaim the pieces—and the peace—they had lost along the way.

A successful surgeon in the group shared that although he was at the top of his career, he felt numb and had been plagued for years with treatment-resistant depression. There was the sporty teacher from the Midwest whose husband had died of a sudden heart attack, leaving her a widow in her early forties. There was a graduate student who was there to gather research for an article but who also carried deep anger and wounds from a challenging relationship with her alcoholic mother. And then there was Rose, who hadn't yet said a word.

Rose was like a dam ready to burst. Her pent-up pain was palpable. As she spoke, she wrung her hands and kept her gaze on the ground. She shared that she was just over a year out of a 30-year marriage to a very successful and prominent executive, who had been her abuser. She described her husband as a man who was highly respected in the community but a complete monster to her behind the scenes. She was careful not to give any information that would identify him, but we all sensed he was someone we may have heard of. The way she protected his identity gave me the feeling she was still fearful of him. Finding the courage and strength to leave him and her marriage was the hardest thing she had ever done. She described getting out of the marriage as "escaping" and talked about how she had completely lost herself after years of his narcissistic abuse. At this point, she covered her face in her hands and sobbed deeply. The group was silent. We all felt her pain.

After a few minutes, she lowered her hands from her face. "I am here to try to find myself again and reclaim all the parts of myself I have lost along the way. I hope it isn't too late for me to come back to life."

> Every journey invites your inner guide to facilitate your healing.

How our inner guidance and inner-healing intelligence shows up is as unique as the person journeying and as the healing they need. Rose needed to heal her heart and reconnect to herself and her own personal power. Her openness to receive, return, and reclaim was a perfect mindset for her journey.

I was assigned to Rose as her primary facilitator on journey day. I had secretly hoped we would be paired, as I felt a deep compassion for her situation. I wanted to support her in the process of reclaiming her power and her life. I wanted this not only for Rose and her individual healing but also symbolically for all the women who had been diminished by men. I believe our individual healing sparks an element of collective healing.

The next day—with intentions explored and expressed, and preparations completed—the group of nine perfect strangers took their mushrooms together and then headed off to the spots they had set up for their journeys. Rose and I walked to a corner of the property, where she had set up a chaise lounge with blankets in the shade of a palm tree. This was to be her cozy spot to journey for the day. I had a blanket on the ground next to her, where I would sit quietly, attuned and attentive.

As Rose settled in, she told me she had hoped I would be her guide because she felt a safety with me that she couldn't explain. It seemed we were meant to work together that day.

Rose settled behind her eye mask, with her headphones and the ambient soundtrack leading her into a non-ordinary state. For the first hour, her body was restless and agitated. Once or twice, at her request, I placed my hand gently on her shoulder…each time she settled, reassured by my presence.

A few times, I heard her mumble that she didn't want to do this, and I heard her say "GET AWAY" in a very distressed voice. This led to several hours of heaving sobs. She went through two boxes of tissues as she released all the stored pain and sadness that she had been carrying for years.

At some point, her crying turned to words. I could make out a soft and soothing whisper of "Thank you, thank you…"

About four and a half hours after Rose had consumed her mushrooms, she sat up and removed her tear-drenched eye mask. Eyes swollen from crying, mascara smudged, she asked me to help her to the bathroom.

In a quiet voice, she said, "It's all so beautiful, even the darkness."

She leaned against me a bit, tired from all she had been through that day and in the years leading up to that moment.

Not wanting to engage her in too much dialogue, I responded with a simple but sincere "Yes, it is."

When we got back to her spot, she told me she needed to sit directly on the grass. She put her headphones back on, and I moved out of sight to give her space. She leaned back on the grass, arms outstretched. Then she laughed, cried, and smiled for another hour. I could sense that much had transpired, transforming Rose, and I was excited for her and her healing.

That night, the guests all had a quiet evening and were encouraged to journal, rest, and recover.

After a journey, we encourage participants to stay reflective and let the experience of the day just settle over them. The next morning, we all reassembled in our circle for the integration session. Sharing their experiences, holding space for each other and their respective healing, is a beautiful and powerful time. The facilitators skillfully help each guest tease out the key insights and information from their journeys that they can use to heal, rewire, and recalibrate heart and mind. It is always amazing to bear witness to these powerful and provocative experiences.

When Rose, who had been so reserved before, raised her hand to share her journey experience first, the whole group was surprised. Tears began to flow down her face before she had even uttered her first word. Through her tears, Rose recounted how her journey had begun, feeling very dark and scary, and she had wanted desperately for it to stop. She feared giving up control and being swept away into the darkness. She had felt as though she was surrounded by a large and threatening group of male figures—pushing her, shoving her, and knocking her down. She couldn't identify them, but she felt small and insignificant, like they were pushing past her as if she wasn't even there.

She remembered when I had put a hand on her shoulder and told her she was safe. She said in that moment, the men disappeared, and she was transported up what seemed like a few levels or floors higher. In this new realm, she was surrounded by various women of all ages, many of whom she recognized from different periods of her life. As she encountered each one, they reminded her of a part of herself she had shared with them. And in that moment, those parts of her were reclaimed, and she remembered and re-embraced each of them.

She saw an old roommate from college, and they laughed together. The friend expressed a deep gratitude to Rose for the time they had spent being free spirits, full of promise. In that encounter, the playful part of Rose returned to her. She felt it find its way back into her being in an embodied way she couldn't describe. She said she was overcome with gratitude for finding these parts, and she remembered saying "thank you" over and over.

But she said the most powerful part of her journey came at the end when she lay down on the grass. As she rested her body on the ground, she had a strong and very real sensation of the earth holding her like a hug and heard a beautiful voice whisper, *Let me take those chains off you that have held you back. Feel the lightness and be free.*

She knew it was Mother Earth, or some great divine feminine power, speaking to her. She felt her body wrapped in heavy chains, and she recognized that they symbolized all the ways she had been dominated and belittled by her ex-husband. As the voice whispered, the earth beneath her opened up and swallowed the chains, pulling them down deep below the surface. Then just as suddenly as it had opened, the earth closed back up.

In that moment, Rose felt her whole body fill with a lightness of being that she had not felt since childhood.

"I can't even begin to explain it. It was like Mother Earth pulled all the pain, shame, grief, and regret from my heart and soul and placed me gently back on the ground, healed."

As Rose finished sharing her journey, there was barely a dry eye in the group. Everyone was touched by her vulnerability. She then shared that the reason she had raised her hand to go first was because for the past 30 years, she had never been first, never been heard, and never allowed to take up space. So this was her first new act of reclaiming her space, her power, and her voice.

The whole group clapped, and a few people even gave her a standing ovation. That bold new way of being, witnessed and supported by everyone, was healing medicine in and of itself. Rose reclaimed so much on her journey. She found lost parts of herself and stepped back into her power. She could see a path ahead, and now—freed from the chains that had held her back—she could travel more lightly. It was time for Rose to fly.

USING PSILOCYBIN TO RECOVER FROM NARCISSISTIC ABUSE

A professionally guided psilocybin session held in a safe setting can offer a profound path to healing if you are recovering from narcissistic abuse. This experience often leaves you with deep wounds—eroded self-worth, chronic self-doubt, and an internalized narrative shaped by manipulation and gaslighting. Psilocybin works by quieting your brain's default mode network, loosening rigid thought patterns, and creating space for fresh perspectives. In this expanded state of awareness, you can begin to see yourself with clarity and compassion, disentangling your identity from the distorted lens of the abuser. The experience can reconnect you to your inner strength and a sense of self that predates the trauma, while fostering deep emotional release and forgiveness—not to excuse the harm done, but to free yourself from its grip. Integration practices after the session can help anchor these insights, rebuilding a foundation of self-trust, empowerment, and resilience.

INTEGRATION PRACTICES FOR HEALING FROM AN ABUSIVE RELATIONSHIP

Integration, recovery, and reclamation begin with compassionate and supportive therapy centered on validating the survivor's experience. Rose's journey of recovery would involve rebuilding self-trust and gently releasing her internalized shame. Somatic practices, parts work (like IFS), breathwork, and trauma-informed mindfulness would help reconnect Rose to her body and reset her nervous system to a sense of safety.

Building on the imagery that had presented on Rose's journey, I created a guided meditation where she would lie on the earth and imagine feeling Mother Nature absorbing all her hurt, shame, and self-doubt. As she imagined the earth pulling those negative emotions and beliefs into the soil to be absorbed, she was also lifted by the light and sky and given the gift of "lightness of being." This guided meditation would help her reconnect to that embodied feeling and the received message of release and rebirth that had come to her so beautifully on her journey.

Rose's psychedelic journey gave her deep soul healing and a path to reclaim her voice, her intuition, and her sacred sense of self. Healing is not just about recovering from abuse—it's about rising back into wholeness.

Try the following practices for recovering from abusive relationships:

- **Boundary Mapping:** Enumerate your emotional, physical, and energetic boundaries. Make a column for each of these areas, and list what you will not allow—the treatment, words, behavior (physical or emotional) that are not acceptable to you. Rehearse saying them aloud. Get clear on what you will and will not allow in your life. You get to make the rules, not anybody else.

- **Mirror Work:** Speak daily affirmations to your reflection: "You are enough. You are free." It may sound silly, but this can be powerful. Pay attention to how you talk to yourself. Do not let your abuser's voice continue in your head. Become your best friend and biggest champion. Have your internal dialogue be a strong, supportive, and loving voice that always has your back.

- **Cord-Cutting Ritual:** Write a letter to your abuser and say it ALL. Now burn that letter, and imagine as it burns that you are freed from carrying that anger, sadness, regret, and shame.

- **Reclaiming Playlist:** Create a music mix that activates your power and joy. This is the soundtrack of your salvation. Crank it in your car and rock out to it loudly, proudly, and unapologetically. For those of you in my generation, think Helen Reddy's "I Am Woman."

Journaling Prompts

1. Have you ever been in a relationship that caused you to shrink, play small, or feel like you were less than?

2. What part of you allowed this to happen? Who is she, and what was she afraid of?

3. What part of you found the strength to leave and save yourself? Describe her and how you support her.

4. What does it mean to you to have personal power?

5. How did other women support you in reclaiming your power, and how do you support other women so they can stand in their power?

CHAPTER 6

The Missing Piece for Peace

> There is a voice that doesn't use words. Listen.
>
> — RUMI

There is a good chance you have experienced some trauma and tragedy in your life. These are inescapable parts of the human experience. Divorce, relationship challenges, death of loved ones, disease, depression, and anxiety are losses and lashes that can leave you with profound emotional wounds that are often invisible to others. Your grief may manifest not only as sadness but also as numbness, anxiety, anger, insomnia, or a lingering sense of emptiness and disconnection.

For some, the grieving process becomes complicated by trauma, particularly when the loss was sudden, violent, or unresolved.

These emotional burdens can affect every area of your life, including relationships, mental health, physical wellbeing, and your sense of purpose.

Amanda came to me to heal one area of her life but found that a deeper, older wound needed more of her attention and intention for healing.

AMANDA'S JOURNEY

Anyone who met Amanda would describe her as bright and bubbly. She wore colorful clothes, had an infectious smile, and spoke with an enthusiastic tone. But looks can be deceiving. And in Amanda's case they were. When she reached out to me by email, she said she was looking for support in becoming more present in her life. She hoped psilocybin could help her become more mindful, present, and playful.

Almost as a side note, she mentioned that her mother had died when she was young, but Amanda felt she had dealt with that sufficiently through years of therapy. She was interested in a psilocybin experience primarily to explore a current unexplained and unwelcome "flatness" she was feeling in her life.

A few days later, we connected on a video call. As Amanda and I spoke about her intentions for her psilocybin journey, she again said she was feeling flat and numb and not terribly excited about things. She hoped a journey would help lift this fog and illuminate the cause of her emotional numbness. I asked if she was comfortable sharing a bit about her mother's death. She said she had spent years and years working through that loss in therapy and felt it had been well processed. She disclosed that her mother had been hit by a car in front of her when she was 10 years old. I didn't push for any more details, and she presented it as well-packaged and processed trauma, but I wondered if this significant life event might show up in her journey. However, I followed her lead, as she clearly preferred to focus on her current emotional state.

She couldn't really identify anything that was triggering her feelings of disconnection. She had a solid marriage, a rewarding job, and two kids she enjoyed. She framed her intention as being open and curious to receive any insight that could support her in reclaiming her joy and her ability to feel fully present with herself and the world around her. She was hoping this journey would help her reconnect to a lightness and joyfulness so she would not have to consider antidepressants, which her primary care provider had suggested.

Her preparation included learning how to calm herself in case the journey triggered anxiety. We worked on some breathing activities, a calming mantra, and how to reach out so I could be there with a hand on her shoulder as reassurance and grounding. I reminded her to be curious and not fearful and to approach everything that presented with an open curiosity.

The journey took place in a quiet cabin tucked into an aspen grove. A small stream babbled nearby. Amanda felt relaxed and unplugged from the responsibilities of her busy daily life. We mixed her tea, and she settled into her chair to listen to the soothing music she had selected, designed for this therapy.

Her last comment to me before going into her journey was "I'm curious but also a bit skeptical. If I'm going to get signs, they're going to need to be really loud and obvious."

Amanda settled behind her eye mask and drifted off into her journey. She was deep in her experience for about four and a half hours and never indicated needing support, though at one point when she was sobbing intensely, I placed my hand gently on her shoulder. At hour five, she came out of the medicine and was returning to her normal consciousness. She sat up, walked slowly to the bathroom, and then asked to have some time to journal before we spoke. I sat in the living room and waited for her to join me.

An hour later, she came with journal in hand and sat next to me. Her first words were "That was incredible and so unexpected."

As Amanda relayed her experience, it seemed that much of her journey was rather light and playful. She said she felt like the mushrooms had invited her to join them in a magical, mystical forest, and they revealed to her how everything is alive, including the rocks, trees, and flowers.

She said, "I could feel the energy of everything." This filled her with a sense of awe and excitement. "Little bugs spoke to me, the leaves whispered, and everything had something interesting to tell me." She was giddy and giggling as she told me about this adventure.

I asked her how she felt.

She looked at me wide-eyed and said, "Light and joyful."

I pointed out that her brain was just rewired for being light and joyful having just had that embodied experience. Amanda said that experience was exactly what she needed to pull her back into the present moment with a renewed sense of wonder and presence. Even sitting with me there in the living room, she felt a heightened sense of interconnectedness to the plants and the light and shadows dancing on the floor.

Everything felt alive and interesting, which made her feel so much more alive and interested. She was eager to bring this newfound lightness of being with her out into the world and to share it with her husband and sons.

I was thrilled with the way this mushroom journey had spoken to Amanda's intention and desire to remember and reconnect with the magic in the moment. Had that been the extent of her journey, I would have considered it a huge win for emotional wellbeing—but there was another experience that was equally, if not more, impactful.

Amanda said, "Remember how I said I would need a really loud and obvious sign? Well, they gave me one."

"About what?" I asked.

Her voice softened and she told me this.

> I found myself standing and looking out across a vast meadow with a clear, blue sky above. I sensed something important was going to happen, but I didn't know what. I felt calm and exquisitely alert.
>
> Suddenly, I was aware of a presence behind me. I felt a woman's hands on my shoulders, and I could smell my mother's perfume. The scent cascaded me into a sea of memories of my beautiful, loving mom. Then she whispered in my ear, "Forgive…" I looked up to the sky and saw the sign: Clouds spelled out the word FORGIVE.

In that moment, Amanda realized she had always been angry at her mother for leaving her. In all the years of therapy, no one had ever helped her connect with and work through the deep anger she carried toward her mother for leaving her. But here, deep in her journey, the permission to forgive was lovingly and tenderly delivered by her mother. Amanda could feel the deeply buried rage and anger come up and pass through her as it alchemized into a profound, full heart, mind, and soul feeling of overwhelming forgiveness and love for her mom.

As Amanda forgave her mother, she felt herself released from the heavy weight and burden of all the unexpressed anger she had been carrying. She felt the forgiveness emanate from her body through to her mother. That last piece of Amanda's healing around her mother's death brought a missing peace to her heart and soul.

As part of Amanda's integration, I suggested she find or make a literal sign that she could put in her house somewhere that read "FORGIVE." When I had a follow-up integration call with Amanda a month later, she shared that a week after her journey, she had gotten a tattoo of the word FORGIVE on her shoulder, right where she had felt her mother's hand. This seemed a most fitting way to honor and connect with that beautiful moment and healing.

She had also followed the lead from her journey and began spending time outside, playing like a kid in the woods. The paths she had used to hike mindlessly she now explored mindfully, attuned to the bugs and plants and play of light and shadow. This new mindful presence amplified her sense of calm and increased her ability to be more present and connected to those around her. Amanda's journey brought about healing that had ripple effects out to her relationship with her husband and kids.

Our peace is often the missing piece to being present.

USING PSILOCYBIN FOR PROCESSING LOSS

Psilocybin-assisted therapy is emerging as a promising approach to help individuals process and heal from profound grief and traumatic loss. Clinical research currently underway suggests that psilocybin can facilitate emotional breakthroughs by allowing individuals to revisit and reframe their grief from a place of expanded awareness and deepened compassion. In studies at Johns Hopkins, participants in psilocybin research indicated the experience was often one of the most profound and mystical experiences of their lives.[16] These experiences create a renewed sense of connection to their lost loved ones, spiritual insights, and a shift from despair to acceptance. The medicine appears to quiet the default mode network of the brain, often associated with rumination, while opening a space for profound emotional release and meaning-making.

> When experienced in a safe, therapeutic setting, psilocybin can allow women to move through grief with greater grace, helping them reclaim vitality, peace, and a sense of inner continuity beyond the loss.

Amanda's journey returned her to her kids and husband and connected her to a lost part of herself and her peace, which in turn increased her ability to be more present.

INTEGRATION PRACTICES FOR PROCESSING LOSS

Integration therapy for clients who have used psilocybin to heal traumatic loss involves helping them process grief in a more spacious, compassionate, and embodied way, while guiding the brain and nervous system toward new patterns of meaning, connection, and emotional regulation. Psilocybin often allows individuals to reach into the depth of their sorrow with less resistance and more love, sometimes reconnecting them with the presence of their lost ones or accessing spiritual insights about death, impermanence, and continuation.

In the neuroplastic window following the journey, clients are uniquely positioned to reframe their relationship to loss, soften the grip of traumatic memory, and begin integrating their grief as a part of their story rather than their whole identity. Integration practices during this time can help anchor these shifts and reinforce neural pathways of resilience, reverence, and emotional flexibility. Amanda's story is a wonderful example of how our inner intelligence finds the parts that need to be healed, even when they are buried deep below the surface.

Try the following exercises for integrating loss:

- **Letter to the Lost One:** Write a heartfelt letter to the person or part of life that has been lost, expressing anything left unsaid. Read it aloud as you envision that person receiving your words. Then burn your letter, imagining you are released from all you expressed as the words fall to ashes.

- **Somatic Grief Release:** Practice a gentle body-based grief movement—such as rocking, humming, or breathwork with vocal toning—to move emotion through the body and regulate the nervous system. Find a tone or frequency that you can imagine is alchemizing your pain and grief into healing energy.

- **Sacred Object or Altar Creation:** Create a small altar or sacred space with items that represent your loss, transformation, and healing. Use it as a grounding point for daily reflection, gratitude, and connection.

Journaling Prompts

1. What did I feel, see, or understand about my loss during my journey that I want to remember?

2. If I could speak with the person I lost, what would I say? What might they say to me?

3. What does honoring this loss—and still choosing to live fully—look like for me now?

CHAPTER 7

Taking a Quantum Leap

> There are losses that rearrange the world. Deaths that change the way you see everything, grief that tears everything down, pain that transports you to an entirely different universe, even while everyone else thinks nothing has changed.
>
> — MEGAN DEVINE

Some of the most meaningful and profound work I have done has been supporting women on their healing journey after losing a child. Suffering this loss to a drug overdose or suicide is a grief that defies words—a shattering of the soul that can leave you suspended in unbearable sorrow and guilt.

Psilocybin can soften the edges of trauma and open a profound space for healing by facilitating emotional release, spiritual connection, and a reweaving of meaning into a space that seems meaningless. Many of my clients who have experienced this therapy report an embodied sense of contact with their child, experiences of forgiveness, and moments of peace that are indescribably transcendent. By quieting your inner critic and accessing a deep well of compassion, psilocybin helps you move through paralyzing grief toward integration, where love remains.

Olivia's story illuminates how this medicine can not only heal us but also transport us beyond the definitions and boundaries of life and death.

OLIVIA'S JOURNEY

Olivia's 18-year-old son died by accidentally ingesting a fentanyl-laced antidepressant given to him by a friend, a tragedy that all too often impacts families across America. According to the National Center for Health Statistics, overdose deaths due to fentanyl saw a steady increase year over year this century[17]. Olivia never anticipated her life would become entwined in such a tragic statistic. The pain of this loss completely upended her world.

When Olivia reached out to me, she had already spent three years on antidepressants and had been through three different therapists and numerous support groups in an effort to alleviate the gripping grief that consumed her. She was haunted by the experience of finding her only child dead in his room the night before he was to start his junior year of high school. She could not move beyond the horror and pain of that moment. She had become reclusive and pulled away from friends and activities that used to bring her pleasure. She spent her days in her son's room looking at his art and journals for hours on end. He had been a bright and curious boy filled with questions and curiosity about quantum physics, philosophy, and metaphysics. She missed the hours they spent engaged in conversations about these topics. There was a deep connection between them grounded in pondering these bigger existential questions about the universe. She missed his body, mind, and soul so much. Every day felt like the first day after his death, even through years had passed.

One day, as she was getting her antidepressants refilled, her psychiatrist shared the research she had read on the effectiveness of psilocybin for coping with grief and loss, and she suggested perhaps this would be something for Olivia to try. Her psychiatrist told her that she could access this treatment legally and safely in Colorado and offered to help her find a qualified therapist.

Eager for a new path to heal her heart, Olivia agreed, and with a bit of web searching, they found me. For many years, she had been interested in trying a psychedelic experience as a means of exploring her own consciousness and the quantum field. And now it felt right to use this path to seek psycho-spiritual and soul healing as well. The antidepressants numbed her pain, but they also numbed her mind. She wanted to find a new path back to herself, her heart, and her wholeness. She wanted to learn to live with her loss without losing herself.

I met Olivia via several Zoom sessions in the month preceding her session. Over those weeks, we discussed her grief and the beautiful relationship she'd had with her son, her only child. She spoke of his amazing ethereal art and how his drawings and writings spoke of a world and beings beyond this human plane. She had loved fostering his curiosity and her own by finding books they could share on metaphysics and the mystical. They had spent hours discussing podcasts and books, and shared this unusual interest in the unknown.

In losing her son, Olivia had also lost her best friend. Her hope for this psilocybin journey was simply to find an incremental easing of her pain. She had realistic expectations and knew that no outcome was guaranteed, but she also needed to try something new.

The day Olivia arrived for her session, all the pain she was carrying showed on her face. She was a beautiful woman with a very stylish haircut that came just to her shoulders. But her features were filled with a soul pain that could be read in her eyes and in her energy. She arrived at our session with several framed photos of her handsome son and an armload of his drawings and journals. As she walked through the door, his presence was very much with her.

"Shortly after my son died," she said, "I began to have vivid dreams where it seemed like he was very clearly speaking to me, like he was right there with me."

In the dreams, he directed her to his art or journals and would point out amazing little synchronicities. One of his doodles depicted him ascending through a cloud with numbers and calculations.

"The calculations were about space and time, and the numbers reflected the day he died," she told me. She paused and looked up to see my reaction.

I assured her that because I worked with psychedelics and the mystical, nothing surprised me. "I am a believer in the mystery that exists beyond what we think we know."

A wide and almost mischievous smile stretched across her face.

She continued. "In these dreams, he was telling me he moved beyond space and time when he died. He had done this doodle two years before his death!"

She handed me one of his drawings—an image of what can only be described as another dimension. Numbers and calculations encircled his head, and in his hands were two numbers, the month and day he had passed. Goosebumps ran up and down my spine. I was glad Olivia had found me to do this work, as I cast no judgment on her and, in fact, was equally intrigued by the unexplainable experiences she was bringing forward.

She wondered if her psilocybin journey would be similar to these powerful dreams she had been having, given that dreams are a non-ordinary state of consciousness, as is the psychedelic state. Her lifelong curiosity about the metaphysical realm and consciousness, combined with her son's premonitions, created an ideal mindset for her journey. She had no fear, just boundless curiosity and hope for healing some of her persistent grief.

We spoke for about an hour about how she could lean in to trusting her inner-healing intelligence and how to believe in the medicine and release into the experience. Olivia felt prepared and hopeful for the journey. She placed her son's journals, art, and photographs on the table beside the bed. She drank her mushroom tea, put on her eye mask and headphones, and dropped quickly into her journey. About a half an hour into the journey, I sat across the room watching as she became very animated and vocal. She was repeating her son's name loudly and excitedly, like she was greeting him.

She laughed boisterously and yelled things like "Oh yes, yes, I see! I get it!"

For most of the five hours she was on her medicine journey, she giggled like a little girl.

I helped her to the bathroom once, and she just kept saying, "This is so amazing. I want to hurry and get back in."

The sheer joy I was witnessing was a complete 180 from the depressed presentation she had come in with.

When she came out of her journey, she was bubbly, effusive, and eager to tell me all that she had just experienced. Before she began, she gave me a huge hug and thanked me.

Her first words were "I don't think I can explain what just happened, but it was the most amazing and beautiful experience I have ever had in my entire life—and the really amazing part is that I shared the whole adventure with my son."

Once again goosebumps ran up and down my spine, and I felt tears well up in my eyes.

The women who journey on psilocybin are not escaping reality—they are entering a deeper one. One that holds the sacred map and eternal secrets of their souls.

Olivia relayed how her son had suddenly been there in the room with her in a way that felt totally real and grounded. He appeared as if sitting with her on the bed and told her how he had left this life because his next level of learning about the universe couldn't be done in his human form. He then proceeded to share quantum physics and metaphysical knowledge with her that she had somehow been able to understand, but in a way she couldn't articulate. He kept tossing truths and insights at her, causing her whole body to have this warm rush like some sort of kundalini energy wave.

As she continued to share her journeys with me, her eyes were wet with tears of joy. "He was being his usual self and doing all of this with his unique humor. He made me laugh so much!"

She went on to relate more of the wisdom he had imparted. "He explained big existential concepts such as why humans had created religion, why we have wars, and how death is just a shifting of energy from one plane to another."

All the concepts and conversations had resonated deeply with her and brought her clarity and calm. At one point, she told him she was sorry she wouldn't get to see him grow into a man. He smiled and laughed and began to toss her Polaroids of himself at different ages, growing older.

She said that made her really happy and was so in keeping with his humor. I felt so much joy radiating from her as she shared these experiences. We were both aware that no science could explain this experience, nor did we need it to.

We spoke about her journey for almost two hours. She savored every moment recalling the time she had just spent in that other realm of consciousness, close and connected to her son. She had so much peace in her heart that it felt like she had a new relationship with her son that continued beyond this space and time.

I don't dare make claims that I can help people communicate with deceased loved ones, but I also hold space for the great unknown, and that may be what happened for Olivia. What I do know is that her experience was profoundly meaningful for her and brought healing that talk therapy and pharmaceuticals could not. Her journey helped her reclaim her quality of life, and that is what matters most. She felt like she had a new relationship with her son that allowed her to accept his loss from this worldly plane and helped her to connect with him in a different way.

In a one-year follow-up call, she reported a sustained decrease in her depression and an increased engagement in her quest for knowledge about consciousness and metaphysics. In her dreams, she continues to connect with her son and finds great peace in her new perspective on death as a transition to another plane. She was excited to share with me that since her initial experience, she was able to come off her antidepressants, able to feel a full range of emotions again, and could manage her grief, as it now sat side-by-side with her joy.

Olivia has already made plans to return for another journey to support her continued healing.

USING PSILOCYBIN TO HELP HEAL FROM AN UNBEARABLE LOSS

Psilocybin therapy is showing remarkable promise in helping parents navigate the depths of complicated grief—the kind that occurs after losing a child in a sudden and traumatic way[18]. In the safe container of a therapeutic setting, psilocybin can soften the edges of trauma and open a profound space for healing by facilitating emotional release, spiritual connection, and a reweaving of meaning. Many who undergo this therapy report a sense of contact with their child, experiences of forgiveness, and moments of peace that feel transcendent.

By quieting the inner critic and accessing a deep well of compassion, psilocybin helps bereaved parents move through paralyzing grief toward integration—where love remains, and life, though forever changed, can begin again with purpose and hope.

Olivia's psilocybin session brought her even more hope and healing than she could have wished for. Her experience helped her redefine her perspective on death and gave her a new way to be in a relationship with her departed son. Psycho-spiritual healing of the highest order.

INTEGRATION PRACTICES FOR CHILD LOSS

The powerful integration practices I've included here support your journey through grief after the loss of a child, particularly following a psilocybin-assisted grief therapy session. These exercises are designed to honor the heightened emotional openness and neuroplasticity you experience in the weeks following a psilocybin session. Each of these practices will help you metabolize and alchemize the deep emotions stirred by the psilocybin journey and the loss itself—supporting a gradual shift from pain to peace, from rupture to relationship with your child in spirit.

- **Somatic Grief Release Through Restorative Touch and Breathwork:** Grief is stored in the body, often as tightness in the chest, throat, or solar plexus. A gentle somatic practice can help release stored sorrow and restore a sense of connection to self.
    1. Lie on your back with one hand over your heart and the other on your belly.

2. Breathe deeply and rhythmically into the heart space.

3. As feelings arise, allow gentle movement or sound (sighing, humming, weeping) to flow without judgment.

This can be done alone or with a somatic therapist or bodyworker trained in trauma-informed care.

- **Writing to the Spirit of Your Child:** Following a psilocybin session, many parents report feeling a deep, ongoing connection to the spirit of their child. Writing can help sustain and evolve this connection in healthy ways.

    1. Begin by lighting a candle or placing a photo nearby.

    2. Then write a letter *to* your child. Say what's in your heart, what you miss, what you are grateful for.

    3. Next, allow yourself to write a letter *from* your child to you, imagining what their soul might want you to hear.

This sacred dialogue often brings great comfort and insight.

- **Ritual of Release and Reconnection:** A personal ritual can symbolically release unresolved pain, while anchoring an ongoing bond in love rather than loss.

    1. Choose a meaningful location—by water, under a tree, or in a garden.

    2. Bring an object (a stone, flower, or piece of paper with a message) that represents your grief or guilt.

3. Offer it to the earth, fire, or water with an intentional release.

4. Let the heavy grief be alchemized as you call in a greater energy of love and connection.

5. Plant something, create a small altar, or wear a symbolic token to represent your continued connection in love, beyond form.

Grief does not keep you connected to the one you have lost—love and joy do.

- **Artmaking as Medicine:** After a psilocybin journey, creating visual art can help externalize and transform complex emotions. Use collage, painting, clay, or even simple drawing to express aspects of your journey—your grief, visions, moments of connection, and transformation. Let it be process-oriented, not product-focused. Making art can help you express what words often cannot.

Journaling Prompts

Reflect on a moment in your life when pain—emotional, physical, or spiritual—brought you to your knees. Revisit the memory gently, without rushing to fix or judge it.

1. Ask "What has my pain taught me about my strength, my boundaries, or my deepest needs?"

2. Now imagine that pain as raw material, like lead in the hands of an alchemist. Write about what it would take to transmute that experience into gold. Ask yourself…

- "What qualities—wisdom, resilience, clarity, purpose—emerged from the fire of that suffering?"
- "How am I different now because of it?"

3. Ask "What part of my pain has become a source of my power, and how can I honor the transformation it offers me?"

CHAPTER 8

Remembering the Light of Love

> The wound is the place where the Light enters you.
>
> — RUMI

Your losses shape you. Prolonged grief after the loss of a young child or a lingering illness like cancer can leave you drowning in a dark and deep sea of despair, unable to even reach the hands that try to pull you up. The trauma of watching a child suffer and die often leads to profound existential distress and disconnection between partners, as each carries their own private pain, emotionally stranded from each other—stuck in a loop of sorrow, helplessness, and isolation that strains even the strongest relationships. It can be a very lonely journey that seems like it has no end.

These were the difficult emotions that consumed Corrine when I met her on that crisp fall day in October 2025.

CORRINE'S JOURNEY

I first met Corrine, a beautiful woman in her thirties, outside on a grassy knoll. It was a gorgeous fall day with a bright blue sky and the lightest of cool breezes. Corrine and I immediately felt comfortable in each other's company, as if we had known each other for years.

But having lost her two-year-old to cancer, the beautiful day we shared was just another painful one in her world profoundly changed by grief. Pain weighed down her shoulders and lined her face. She shared that for the last two years, her grief had made it hard for her to even breathe at times. It made even the most basic daily tasks almost too difficult to manage. Her bed had become her only safe space, which left her other children and husband alone to manage their grief without her. She knew something had to change and that somehow and someday, she would need to reemerge into the world and rejoin her family and her life.

Corrine and her husband decided psilocybin therapy might be worth a try. Even her psychiatrist supported the idea. With a bit of research, she had come across an interview I had recently done on the Psychedelic Medicine Association's podcast about psilocybin-assisted therapy for grief and loss. It was exactly the information and connection she had been searching for.

Corrine called me and was surprised when I answered after two rings. In that moment, I felt compelled to answer, which was not typical of me. I almost always let calls go to voicemail. The crossing of our paths felt like it was meant to be.

As we prepared for her session, she told me all about her son and the horrible, challenging last year of his life, how he had been so sick and in and out of the hospital.

"I felt so helpless and useless that I couldn't save my little boy, couldn't protect him from all the pain or from death."

She sobbed for a few minutes and then looked straight into my eyes. "I'm not sure I will ever be whole or happy again, and no one understands this."

To say her son's death had left her devastated was an understatement.

Grief lingers in the doorway like an uninvited guest, refusing to leave until it's sure you have heard every story it carries. It becomes a part of us forever.

Corinne needed to change her relationship to her overbearing grief so she could return to her life among the living, which was a daunting challenge. She had two stepsons and a husband who needed her to return to them and to this life. She framed her journey's intention as a reconnection to her husband and sons. She hoped to find a way to hold her son who had passed in her heart but return to her living family. I told her that I too would hold that intention for her journey and her healing.

Corrine prepared the room for her session with great love and tender care. At her bedside, she placed photos of her son, her husband, and her surviving two sons. She unfolded a quilt made of pieces from her son's clothes. Tiny jean pockets, squares of jammies, patches of flannel—all lovingly woven together and covering her like a hug from beyond. As I tucked her in, I imagined her tucking him in.

As she pulled the blanket up and began to lean into the medicine and the music, I said, "I'll be right here if you need me. Just let the music help you flow into the river of the journey."

From behind her eye mask, she asked, "Can you sit and hold my hand for a little while?"

I took her trembling hand in mine. I inhaled a few deep breaths and attuned myself to hold her and her healing with full presence and compassion.

Over the course of her four-and-a-half-hour journey, I watched as Corrine cried and laughed and smiled and sang. The magic of the medicine was doing its thing.

When Corrine started to come out of the medicine and return to her normal consciousness, she was very quiet and lay silently on her bed jotting a few things in her journal. I sat across the room reading a book and allowing her the space to settle back into herself and the here and now. It was hard to read her mood as she was deep in thought, writing in her journal. I suspected it had been a big journey, given all the emotions she had cycled through over the past few hours.

After half an hour passed, Corrine sat up, propped a few pillows behind her back, and called me over to sit next to her. I sat down and gently placed my hand on her arm.

In a very soft voice, I asked, "How was your experience?"

Tears streamed down her face. "He's all right, and he is still here with me. I know that now."

In that moment, with those words, my heart felt like it tripled in size.

She told me that he was with her the minute the medicine kicked in. She couldn't see him, but she could feel his presence and knew they were together—touching, hugging, and connected. "It was so beautiful. He was right there with me, and I could feel him!"

He asked her, "Do you remember the time you and Daddy were dancing in the kitchen before I was born? I was there with you. I was a light inside you. I was light in your heart, and I started growing inside you after that night. I am light in your heart now. That's where I am now, in your heart."

Corrine looked at me. "I had forgotten all about that night, but when he said that, it all came back to me."

She remembered dancing in the kitchen with her husband early in their marriage. They had just decided they wanted to try to have a child of their own, and they danced for what felt like hours and then made love. She realized that was the night she had likely conceived their little one. How could it be that her son was now reminding her about it?

It was such a meaningful memory and image for Corrine, and it brought her so much peace to hear her son tell her that he was in her heart. The healing in that exchange was more powerful than any talk-therapy session or pharmaceutical prescription. It was as compelling as a real interaction.

Corrine said it felt like she'd spent hours with her son—never actually seeing him, but deeply feeling his presence.

He told her "Dance with Daddy more, Mommy. He misses you. I love it when you dance. It makes me really happy."

"It was crazy. He gave me suggestions for how to connect with his brothers and told me they too needed me to help them remember to dance, play, and be happy." He told her she should go to the beach at sunset and sunrise so she could feel him in that light and know that he was always there.

She said he had filled her with a profound sense of knowing that he was safe and okay. He let her know that he was only ever meant to be here for those short two years, but that he was eternal and she should find peace in that. And indeed, that psilocybin session began to bring her peace and heal her broken heart.

I left Corrine that evening to journal and reflect on the powerful experience she'd had. I reminded her not to rush to understand it all and to honor whatever gifts it gave her. That night, she slept well, with a newfound sense of peace sitting close to her tender heart.

Around nine the next morning, I arrived to do more integration with Corrine about her experience. Immediately, I could sense a difference in her energy. She seemed more present, like a part that had been missing had returned. As we continued our conversation from the day before and explored all the elements of her journey, she said it was all so much more than she could have ever imagined. She said it brought her a deep and profound sense of peace. Here's what she told me.

> It was all very, very real. I hadn't expected that. I thought it would be like watching a movie, but it wasn't that at all. It felt as though everything was happening for real and

in this dimension. I don't think I can even really begin to describe it, and I'm sure no one would believe me, but I know that I was absolutely connecting with my son, and that is what matters most to me. A part of me found some peace that I don't think I could have found any other way.

She expressed gratitude for having found me and this path of soul healing. We both acknowledged that we couldn't explain what had happened, nor did we need to try to. But we know she had a beautiful, healing experience that helped her return to the light, the living, and those she loves. Two days after her journey when she was flying home, she described feeling joyful, an emotion she hadn't felt in over three years.

When I checked in with her a month after this journey, she said that while she still felt deep sadness when she thought of her son, she could simultaneously hold feelings of peace and love. She had made it a practice to sit at the beach with her family at sunset and imagine him there with them, feeling his light and love shining on them all. She and her husband now frequently spend nights dancing in the kitchen, with their other kids happily looking on and joining in.

I asked Corrine if I could share a few of her words as a testimonial to help others who were grieving to find this path of healing. She agreed, and I created a post. I was in a hurry and did a quick Google search for an image of a mother and a two-year-old son on a beach. The first image that came up felt perfect.

Just a few minutes after I posted it, Corrine called. "How did you get that picture? I don't remember sending it to you."

I told her it was a random Google image and asked her what she meant.

She immediately texted me a picture of her and her son on the beach. I kid you not, the image was almost identical! Whether science could explain it or not, to us this was another sign from her son letting her know he was here.

The journey brought Corrine's heart hope and healing that had been so elusive since her son's death. It helped her discover a different relationship to her son's loss and helped her alchemize her pain. It sparked the remembrance of the light of love that is in our hearts and keeps us connected eternally.

No one can escape death and loss; these are universal experiences. Perhaps psilocybin therapy can help our hearts find more peace in passings, no matter how painful.

DAN'S JOURNEY

Three months later, Corinne's husband Dan came to see me to have his own experience. In preparing him for his journey, I told him that everyone's encounter is different and that what Corrine had experienced might not be completely different from what he would see or how he would connect with his son. Encouraging people to go in with an open curiosity, trusting that whatever meets them is meant for them, is always my mantra.

Dan's mindset for the journey was trusting that what he needed would come to him. He'd had several of his own recreational experiences with psilocybin in the past, so he was very comfortable with dropping in.

When Dan and I integrated his experience the next day, he was very tearful. He said he was fully in the presence of his son and could feel him and his love in a deeply embodied way. He felt him much as Corrine had and knew he was connecting with him in a very meaningful and healing way. He too was given an understanding that his son was safe and where he needed to be, and that he had played the role he was meant to in the family.

In addition to his profound grief, Dan had also been harboring a terrible guilt that he had not done enough to save his son's life.

"My son somehow put a message in my heart. I know that sounds weird, but that's how it felt. The message was that his death was not my fault and that my love and the way I protected him were some of the most meaningful things he experienced in his two years of life."

As Dan shared this, his body doubled over in deep heaves of sadness. "I can't tell you how important that was for me to hear that from him."

I handed him a box of tissues, and he cried for about 10 minutes. Dan shared with me that this was the first time he had really let himself cry. He had felt like he needed to be strong for his other kids and for Corrine, and that had left no safe space for his own grieving. Allowing himself to experience these emotions was healing for him.

He also had a deep recognition of the beautiful and soulfully connected relationship he had with Corrine. Dan was able to see the gift that both his and Corrine's journeys had given them individually and as a couple. He trusted the psilocybin experience would help Corrine and him create a new spiritual, and shared narrative, about the death of their son and their path forward in healing.

USING PSILOCYBIN TO RECOVER FROM PROLONGED GRIEF AFTER LOSING A CHILD

Emerging research on psilocybin-assisted therapy offers new hope for couples navigating this depth of loss. Studies suggest that psilocybin can reduce the intensity of prolonged grief by quieting the default mode network and allowing for expanded states of consciousness, where emotional insight and forgiveness become possible.[19, 20] In a therapeutic setting, couples often experience a reconnection to themselves, each other, and their shared grief—sometimes even feeling the presence or spirit of their child in ways that bring comfort.

> Psilocybin therapy can foster compassion, reduce blame, and open the door to a more heart-centered healing process, helping couples begin to repair emotional closeness after the unimaginable.

While Corrine and Dan didn't do their sessions together, they still had the benefit of sharing a unique and powerful psychedelic experience, which brought them closer at this very challenging time.

One study in this area is the PARTING trial, an exploratory, open-label pilot study targeting grief in individuals who have lost loved ones to cancer, making it one of the first of its kind. It's not limited to parental grief but does include cancer-related bereavement, which may relate to parents grieving the loss of a child to cancer. The study protocol outlines the therapeutic approach and intentions behind investigating psilocybin's potential benefits in mitigating bereavement-related distress.[21]

INTEGRATION PRACTICES FOR COUPLES AFTER CHILD LOSS

Here are some gentle post-psilocybin integration therapy activities for you and your partner as you work together to heal from the profound grief of losing a child. These practices are designed to support your emotional connection and meaning-making, and to gently repair your bond during the weeks of heightened neuroplasticity following a psilocybin journey. When done with care and intention, these tools can help you and your partner not only survive the unimaginable loss of your child but also gently begin to rebuild your inner and shared world with meaning, memory, and love at the center.

- **Shared Journaling and Storytelling Ritual:** Set aside a regular time to write together or read aloud letters to your child, memories, or reflections from the journey. Share what came up during the psilocybin session and how it continues to unfold, being respectful of each other's differences in perspective and pace.

- **Grief Walks in Nature:** Take regular walks together in nature without needing to talk but just to be side-by-side in quiet companionship. You might choose to dedicate each walk to a memory, emotion, or question you are holding together.

- **Joint Art or Memory Project:** Create a collaborative art piece, photo collage, or memory altar that honors your child and your shared grief journey. This can be deeply grounding and connective, especially if words feel insufficient. It can also be a powerful activity if you have other children who are grieving their sibling.

- **Gratitude and Meaning-Making Rituals:** End each week by sharing one thing you are grateful for or a way your child's spirit or memory has shown up that week. This practice helps shift the focus from only painful memories to ones of shared connection and love. This is also a great activity to do as family with any other children.

Couples Journaling Prompts

1. What did I learn about my grief and my love during the psilocybin journey?

2. How can I show up with tenderness and truth for myself and my partner as we walk this path together?

3. In what ways has grief changed me and us?

4. Are there ways this grief has strengthened us both individually and as a couple?

CHAPTER 9

Navigating the Darkness

> The pain of being aware of your own darkness is one of the most excruciating things one can experience in a lifetime. It feels like dying until it sets you free.
>
> — NZ KAMINSKY

Not all journeys are love, light, and butterflies. Call it shadow work, facing your demons, or having a challenging journey. However you choose to frame it, a little darkness (or a lot) is often a necessary part of the work you must do to heal old wounds and release old scars to move forward. That said, sometimes the set and setting are wrong, the day is off, or you are off. The truth is, psychedelic medicine work is not an exact science, and many variables—what lies within your soul not being the least of them—can impact the experience.

One of my favorite psychedelic researchers, Bill Richards from the Johns Hopkins School of Medicine, uses the analogy of going into the basement with a flashlight to look in the dark corners and face what scares you.[22] This is a wonderful image of how to frame your journey into your own dark places. In our ordinary day-to-day lives, we tend to avoid and push down uncomfortable thoughts and feelings. We do this with alcohol, medication, dissociation, and all manner of distraction. To facilitate our avoidance, we create some well-worn paths and patterns in our brains around avoiding. We literally wire our neural pathways to avoid the uncomfortable.

On psilocybin, in your neuroplastic state, you have increased emotional and psychological flexibility, and it is in this condition that you should approach what you usually avoid so you can create new pathways and patterns, and develop new perspectives about the dark stuff. When I prepare clients for a psilocybin session, I want to be as honest as I can about the fact that they might encounter light and dark, happy and sad, fun and scary material.

You cannot simply dial up the journey you want; you must work with what you get. And occasionally a person gets a very challenging journey.

This was the case with Jen. Her story illuminates how we can find light in the darkness, but it can be a hard and scary trip to get there.

JEN'S JOURNEY

Jen attended an executive women's retreat I facilitated in the beautiful countryside of Portugal. The group was made up of 15 women, all leaders in their various businesses. They had been meeting twice a year for several years. They were very successful women, driven and intentional in building their businesses and their skills as business leaders.

The retreat week was filled with activities such as wine tasting, horseback riding, sound baths, and one supported group psilocybin experience. The leader of the executive group had previously had a psychedelic experience that she felt had greatly enhanced her performance as a team leader. She was eager to offer this to this group and had sought me out for my expertise in psilocybin retreats for mature women. She and I'd had several calls to set the framework for integrating this into the retreat week.

My team and I set up interviews with each of the guests to assess their appropriateness for the experience and prepare them for the psychedelic journey. In Jen's interview, she shared that she'd had a mushroom encounter many years ago in college. It had not been all that pleasant because she'd been at a big concert and got separated from her friends. She expressed trepidation about doing mushrooms again, but also believed that given the professional and safe way they were being done, she thought it could be a good experience. Jen agreed to do the medical screening and said, "Put me on the list. I'm in."

The next month, I would meet her and the rest of the guests in Portugal. The retreat location was stunning. The guests were housed in villas that all faced a beautiful, shaded courtyard with lovely plantings and babbling water features. I felt calm energy the minute I arrived. On Day 3 of the five-day retreat, the guests were excited and nervous about the medicine experience about to unfold.

We all gathered in a large meeting space that had expansive views out across the vineyard. My cofacilitator Monica and I led a preparation session exploring intentions, teaching grounding breathing techniques, and assuring the group of our care and presence with them throughout the session. After a guided meditation, the ladies drank their tea and went to their pre-prepared areas to cozy up and journey.

Monica and I checked in with each guest as they got settled.

I sat down with Jen and asked, "How are you feeling right now? Do you have an intention for your journey?"

She looked at me and took a deep breath. "I don't really have an intention. I guess I feel like I am mostly doing this because the group is. Honestly, I feel a little peer pressure."

This was the first time Jen had shared these thoughts with me, and I wished she had expressed them a bit earlier. But the tea had been consumed, and the journey was forthcoming. I acknowledged her feelings and tried to help her shift to a mindset where this was an opportunity to touch her inner wisdom and see what it might want to share with her. I showed her a few grounding techniques and encouraged her to let the music guide her on a gentle path inward. She seemed to settle into that and lay back, appearing relaxed and comfortable. I made sure to post myself close by to offer her support throughout the day, just in case her journey presented challenges.

Monica and I and two helpers floated about keeping all the guests under a watchful eye. A few needed their hands held as the medicine kicked in. One person needed water, another help getting to the bathroom. All the normal things we deal with as guides. But Jen began to struggle with pretty intense anxiety as her medicine came on. I let the team know I was going to sit with her. I sat on her bed and placed my hand on her shoulder. Her eye mask was up, and her music was off.

"I don't want to do this," she said. "I changed my mind. How can we stop it? I really do not want to do this."

This presented a challenging situation, as there is no Off button. The task now was to help Jen shift into a state of calm so she could release into the experience. We spent half an hour doing some breathing techniques while I held her hand. I encouraged her to just let the music be her guide. She focused on soothing images of places in nature that she loved and being with her husband and two little kids she adored. Her restless distress and fight against the medicine lasted almost an hour. The fatigue from trying to stay in control finally wore her into a state of rest.

For the next three hours, Jen was quiet behind the mask and soothed by the gentle soundtrack that had been curated specially for this group. About every 10 minutes, I would circle back and check on her. Each time, she appeared quiet and relaxed, and her breathing was peaceful. At about hour five, I came into her room and again found her sitting up in bed with her eye mask and music off.

Gently, I asked, "How are you doing? Are you feeling like you have come back?"

She shot me an angry look. "That was the most awful thing I have ever experienced, and I wish I'd never done it! It was terrifying."

My heart sank. While I have no control over what comes up for someone on a journey, I never want it to be so dark that they return in this state. I was committed to helping Jen make sense and meaning of her journey and find her way back to center after this destabilizing experience. I spent the next three hours with her doing just that.

I suggested we move outside to a clearing under a tree. I let her know I would stay with her for as long as she needed me. Despite what appeared to be anger, she was seeking comfort, connection, and grounding. As we sat under the tree, she moved close, pressing up against me, and asked if she could hold my hand. I took her hand in mine and moved in close to her.

In a soft voice, she began to speak. "There was a point when I was rising up through what felt like layers and layers of consciousness or realities. And as I rose, I lost more and more of myself and who I am and what makes me ME. All my earthbound connections fell away and were no longer a part of me. I lost my sense of connection to my kids, my husband, my job, who I am. I was untethered and terrified."

The experience she described is often referred to in psychedelic work as **ego death**, which is a temporary loss or radical loosening of one's usual sense of self—identity, personal boundaries, and the mental framework through which a person experiences the world. This disconnection felt frightening. It severed her from all the things that defined her, including her children, spouse, and earthbound life. She wanted to come back and return to the safety and comfort of those familiar things.

"I had this profound sense of wanting to come back and connect with my kids and my husband and never leave them," she said.

She did have moments of realization that death is an illusion and everything is all just love energy. Those gave her some reprieve from the existential angst of the dissolution of her "self" but not enough to make it a pleasant journey.

She leaned her head against my shoulder and cried. "It all just made me miss my kids and my family. It gave me a greater appreciation for what I have and a recognition that I don't need anything more."

"What a gift that feeling and realization is," I said.

It is often the darkness that sharpens our eyes to the light.

> Darkness doesn't steal the light;
> it teaches us how to see it. How to savor it. How to hold it close.

Only after the storm do we truly notice the softness of the breeze, the warmth of a hand, the miracle of an ordinary day.

In the psychedelic space, there are people who seek out the experience of ego death, but it is not for everyone. With it can come a disconcerting sense of depersonalization, which can take some time and skilled integration to return from.

Jen needed that support to help her get on the path back to her grounding and sense of self. Some lovely insights hidden in her challenging journey were waiting to be discovered. As we spoke, she saw how she had let this group of colleagues influence her decision to join the journey when her initial intuition was that she didn't feel called to the experience. She could see how being among this group of fellow executives often had her putting on a mask and acting in ways that were out of alignment with her true self. The difficulty of the journey gave her this insight in a way that strengthened her desire to be truer to herself and to make choices that best served her.

"I think this experience reminded me that I should always listen to my intuition and not let myself be so influenced by other people."

She also realized that even being on this retreat had gone against her true desire. "I could have spent this week in our cabin in Minnesota with my husband and kids, but I felt some pressure to come on this retreat. I wish I had followed that inner calling. I really do feel like this experience was about remembering to trust my own path and truth more."

As she spoke, I could feel her coming back into herself and her sense of being grounded. These were powerful hard-earned insights.

On the journey, Jen could feel time moving fast, and she had this strong sense of the importance of being present with her kids at this time in their lives. It refocused her perspective and helped her re-examine where she wanted to place her time and attention. She realized she was not truly connected to a path where the focus was climbing the ladder and acquiring more status and money. Her psychedelic experience let her feel the emptiness of that and pulled her with strong emotions back from the beyond to cherish the simple and soulful time here and now with her family and kids.

We spoke for hours under that tree while we plucked blades of grass, watching the shifting shadows and billowy clouds pass by. She realized the big, scary, challenging journey had given her the beautiful gift of knowing, as Dorothy said, "There's no place like home."

FINDING THE BENEFIT IN A CHALLENGING PSYCHEDELIC EXPERIENCE

Research shows that challenging experiences with psilocybin are not uncommon. One of the largest surveys on this topic, published in the *Journal of Psychopharmacology* (2016), found that about 39% of respondents who had taken a high dose of psilocybin described their experience as one of the most psychologically difficult of their lives. However, 84% of those same individuals later reported that the experience ultimately proved to be meaningful or beneficial, even if it was initially distressing.[23]

This highlights the vital importance of set and setting as well as skillful integration. A calm, emotionally supported, and intentional space dramatically reduces the risk of overwhelming fear, confusion, or emotional flooding. Equally important is timing: Choosing to embark on a psilocybin experience because you feel internally ready, not pressured or rushed, is one of the most protective factors. When individuals feel emotionally supported by skilled guides, and have time for preparation and integration, they can meet even the most difficult moments with courage, curiosity, and care—transforming struggle into healing.

Skilled support is essential before, during, and after a challenging session. Integration practices such as somatic, body-centered work, trauma-informed therapy, journaling, movement, and nature immersion help translate the intensity of the experience into insight, resilience, and growth. In this way, even the most difficult journeys can become sacred ground for healing.

When you are healing from a hard psilocybin experience, it is critical that those supporting you are filled with compassion. The pain and fear you experience can be very real and should not be lightly brushed aside.

INTEGRATION PRACTICES FOR DIFFICULT JOURNEYS

The activities suggested here are highly effective for integrating and grounding after a difficult psychedelic journey, particularly when emotions or somatic sensations continue to feel raw or overwhelming. The key is to move slowly, listen to your body, and give yourself the space to metabolize the experience gently and lovingly with skilled support. These practices are backed by trauma-informed and neuroscience-based approaches to support nervous system regulation, emotional processing, and meaning-making. Whether used individually or in combination, these tools help transform intensity into insight and overwhelm into integration. (For further support, see the Additional Resources list at the end of this chapter.)

Using somatic grounding techniques helps you stay centered in your body.

- **Orienting Practice:** Gently turn your head and look around your space, naming what you see, hear, and feel to re-anchor your awareness in the present moment. This can be even further enhanced by being in nature and grounding your senses with the natural elements and surroundings.

- **Weighted Blanket or Body Wrap:** Use a weighted blanket or wrap yourself tightly in a shawl or scarf to provide deep pressure input, which calms the nervous system.

- **Progressive Muscle Relaxation:** Slowly tense and release muscle groups from head to toe to release stored tension and reestablish somatic control.

Regulating your breathing and nervous system can help reduce your anxiety.

- **Box Breathing:** Inhale for 4 counts, hold for 4, exhale for 4, hold for 4. Repeat for several minutes to reduce anxiety and regulate heart rate.

- **Vagus Nerve Stimulation (Humming or Chanting):** Humming or softly chanting activates the vagus nerve and helps return the body to a parasympathetic rest-and-digest state.

Accessing your creativity can be helpful during the integration process. Here are some activities to try.

- **Art Journaling or Intuitive Drawing:** Use color, shape, and images to express what can't yet be spoken. Let your hands reveal what the mind hasn't yet processed.

- **Clay Work or Sculpting:** Working with clay helps externalize internal sensations and provides grounding through tactile engagement.

- **Movement Expression (Dance or Embodied Movement):** Free-form movement, even subtle swaying, allows emotional energy to move through the body and release without needing words.

Aromatherapy and sensory tools can enhance feelings of wellbeing.

- **Essential Oils for Grounding:** Use earthy oils like vetiver, sandalwood, frankincense, or cedarwood on pulse points or in a diffuser to create a sense of safety and stability.

- **Cold Water Splash or Ice-Cube Hold:** A splash of cold water on the face or holding an ice cube helps reset the nervous system, particularly after dissociation or emotional overwhelm.

Being in nature is another helpful integration tool. When you immerse yourself in the natural world, you may feel a sense of awe and connection to something greater than yourself.

- **Nature Immersion / Forest Bathing:** Spend time barefoot on the earth, sit under a tree, or walk slowly through a natural area. Nature is a powerful healer that helps recalibrate the nervous system and instill calm.

- **Creating a Grief or Healing Altar Outdoors:** Build a small altar with natural objects that symbolize what you are releasing and what you are calling in. This is a powerful ritual to close the energetic container of the journey.

Journaling Prompts

Using the three-phase reflection prompt can help you find meaning in your experience.

1. What happened on my journey? (Describe the journey.)

2. What did I feel or see? (Include emotions, imagery, or insights.)

3. What am I learning or taking with me? (Define the meaning and application.)

Additional Resources

- **Fireside Project**
  Psychedelic Peer Support Line: Free, confidential, non-judgmental support for people currently on or processing a psychedelic experience; also offers an integration call-back program.

  US & Canada: Call or text **62-FIRESIDE** (623-473-7433) www.FiresideProject.org

- **Zendo Project [Multidisciplinary Association for Psychedelic Studies (MAPS)]**
  Psychedelic harm reduction and crisis support: Works primarily at events but also offers educational resources on integrating challenging experiences www.ZendoProject.org

CHAPTER 10

Consciously Coming to the End of Life

> End? No, the journey doesn't end here. Death is just another path, one that we all must take.
>
> — **GANDALF,** *RETURN OF THE KING*

No matter what you believe death is, it is a path that we will all walk one day, just as we walked a path into our human existence. Each of us will face our own mortality. Life and love make us vulnerable. Loss and death are inevitable. The existential angst of your own death or losing a loved one is a deep human pain, which is difficult to soothe with pharmaceuticals. It is a pain of the spirit and soul that calls for a different remedy, perhaps the medicine of the mushrooms.

In my own practice, women who undergo psilocybin sessions often experience a deep sense of peace, spiritual connection, and a reorientation of perspective—shifting from fear to acceptance. Many describe a feeling of merging with something greater than themselves, a dissolving of ego boundaries, and a sense of continuity beyond physical death. These mystical experiences appear to play a key role in alleviating the psychological suffering that often accompanies a terminal diagnosis, allowing women to face the end of life with greater courage, meaning, and inner peace. Certainly, in my own dance with a cancer diagnosis, I found this medicine extremely helpful. I also had the honor of supporting my friend Lisa with this medicine as she navigated the last months of her life with terminal cancer.

LISA'S LAST JOURNEY

Lisa walked up to me like a ray of sunshine, a bouncing bobble of blonde curls dancing on her head. She greeted me with a warm, authentic hug like I was a long-lost friend. We found each other through Facebook and realized we shared many mutual connections and had several parallels in our wellness work. We sent a few messages back and forth and just kept hitting on more synchronicities. We decided we absolutely had to meet for coffee. As we chatted over our lattes that sunny summer afternoon, we fell into fast friendship. One of our shared experiences was having breast cancer. Lisa was a few months into a recurrence of hers, and I was a few months out from my double mastectomy.

We lingered over that first coffee and spoke of our pasts, our presents, and our futures. Lisa's beautiful, effervescent personality and energy radiated as she spoke of her family, friends, and hopes for the future, but the twinge of fear was palpable underneath. This led our conversation in the direction of my work with psilocybin for cancer anxiety. I shared my story and the powerful psycho-spiritual healing this medicine had brought me in navigating my own cancer.

Lisa was very open and curious about the healing it might offer her. With her background in wellness, she knew that the mind-body connection was powerful, and that creating greater inner peace could likely benefit her physically and mentally. I told her about a free retreat I was planning for a small group of women with cancer, something I had done every year since my own. I asked if she would like to join us and was thrilled when she said yes.

The retreat took place several months later. By that point, Lisa's cancer had progressed, and her doctors were now trying new meds almost every month to slow the disease. As her cancer grew, so did her fear. She was now living not only with chronic pain in her body but also in her heart and soul.

She came to the retreat with the hope of finding some relief from the anxiety that was robbing her of being more present with herself and her family. There were two other women on the retreat who were also seeking this type of healing for their hearts. One of them was in her twenties, had recently had a double mastectomy, and was currently in remission. A beautiful, vibrant young woman, she struggled with the impact of this surgery on her relationship to her body, beauty, and sexuality. The other woman was in her late thirties, a mother of two young kids. Her sarcoma had occurred twice but was currently in remission. The terror of a third recurrence and the fear of being apart from her children loomed in the shadows of her calm.

The setting for our retreat was a gorgeously decorated farmhouse set on several acres of pasture with an unobstructed view across a field of horses to the foothills and the snow-capped Rockies beyond. Each woman had her own luxurious room with big windows and expansive views. They had all done psilocybin earlier in their lives and brought their own mushrooms to be brewed into tea for their journeys. My role would be to provide the safe and soulful service of harm reduction, supervising and supporting them as they journeyed on their plant medicine.

The women all arrived on Thursday evening, and we connected over a lovely fireside dinner, sharing stories of the ways cancer had infected our bodies, impacted our lives, permeated our peace, and forced us to face our fears. This was not small talk. It was vulnerable and authentic, and it created a safety and setting that would be a medicine unto itself for these women.

When we woke on Friday morning—journey day—a beautiful snow began to fall. It accumulated quickly, draping everything with a glistening cover of winter white. That stillness and quiet that only snow can bring fell gently over the field, the farmhouse, and us. The women all felt the perfection of this day and this weather, which invited them to snuggle up and journey inward.

After a light breakfast, we gathered in a circle to begin our ceremony. I opened with words that came to me and through me.

> As we step into this sacred circle,
> may we lay down the weight of fear
> and lift up the light of trust.
>
> We call in the spirit of the medicine—
> ancient, intelligent, and gentle—

to walk beside us
as a wise companion and humble guide.

We open our hearts to the healing mystery
that breathes through every cell,
trusting that even in illness,
there is wisdom;
even in uncertainty,
there is a path;
and even in pain,
there is the potential for profound peace.

May this medicine awaken
the knowing within us
that we are whole,
we are held,
and we are never alone.

With courage, with grace,
and with one another,
we now surrender to the unfolding.

We trust the journey.
We trust the medicine.
We trust ourselves.

In preparation, I mentioned that I didn't know what would arise for each of them that day, but I did trust that whatever came up would be in service of their healing. I reminded them that psilocybin can give them a new way to walk through difficult times. It couldn't change their external circumstances, but it could change their internal mindsets and influence how they navigated difficult landscapes.

I told them to remember that "what meets you is meant for you" and to journey boldly. "Be curious, not fearful," I said.

We practiced a few grounding breaths to use as comfort if they felt anxiety arise. We went around the circle and listened as the participants shared their intentions and hopes for their journeys.

Lisa hoped the grip of fear would loosen and allow her to feel more peace and presence in the time she had left with her family. "Fear has hijacked my hope," she said tearfully. Her beautiful intention resonated with us all.

As we held each other's intentions, there was a rich moment of soft silence like the snow-covered field. Hope for healing infused the moment. The ladies then raised their glasses, toasted one another, and drank their mushroom tea. They then went to their respective rooms and readied themselves and their spaces for the journey.

Lisa had photos of her husband and sons next to her bed, as well as a stone from a river in Vermont where she had played as a child. She had water, an aromatherapy spray, and a super comfy blanket. She fluffed her pillows, pulled her eye mask down, and settled into the special psilocybin therapy soundtrack that would accompany and guide her. I tucked her in and wished her a good journey, squeezing her hand with reassurance before I tiptoed to the hall, where I would stay attuned all day, offering support to any women as needed.

There was loud laughter from one room, soft sobbing from another. Lisa remained quiet for the first hour. About an hour into her journey, she began to cry and then mumble, "I know, I know." This is what she described as occurring on her journey.

I found myself walking along the banks of a river I knew in my childhood. I was wearing a heavy jacket of armor. It was rusted and dented, and pieces were falling off as I walked. The unbearable weight of it caused my neck and shoulders excruciating pain. I had an awareness that this was the same pain I had from the cancer, but it was now in my neck and bones. I sensed I was a warrior, that I had been wearing and carrying this armor to protect me my whole life, and it had served me well.

I sat down on a rock along the riverbank and rested against my sword. I didn't feel as strong or powerful as I once had been. I felt tired and worn like the rusty metal I wore. I had this sense that it was time to take the armor off and let the battle be over. I felt this as a powerful choice that was mine to make. I had this very moving embodied sense that another adventure awaited me, one that would not require the heavy and cumbersome armor.

As I slipped my arms out of the metal jacket and let it fall to the ground, I felt a lightness, a freedom, a release. My pain subsided. I stood up to stretch, and I could now see farther into the distance. I was struck by what I saw. Ahead beyond the river and through the canyon was a vast and beautiful high meadow. Light filtered down onto the grass and flowers, giving it a luminous glow. Birds soared and circled lazily in the light. A beautiful peace radiated in my heart and soul. I knew in that moment that it would all be okay. I would always be okay.

Tears streamed down her cheeks as she shared these words. She leaned toward me, took my hand, and repeated the words "I am going to be okay."

That evening, the women spoke only briefly about their experiences, choosing instead a quiet, contemplative stillness. With journals open on their laps, they captured fragments of insight and fleeting impressions, allowing the medicine to settle as the intensity of the day gently receded. The silence was tender and grounding—a bridge back into the present moment.

It was not until the following morning, gathered once more in circle, that we created the sacred container for sharing and honoring. What emerged was a tapestry of profoundly personal stories, each one distinct yet woven with common threads of grief, resilience, and renewal. Some women described moving through dark and difficult terrain, touching the raw edges of sadness, fear, and uncertainty. Yet these heavy emotions, charged with energy, found a way to move and release in the safety of the journey. Others spoke of unexpected moments of joy, beauty, and reconnection to a part of themselves untouched by illness—a place of wholeness, strength, and timelessness.

Across their varied paths, each woman had received a gift: the recognition that they were more than a body marked by cancer, more than a diagnosis. In that expanded perspective, they discovered a measure of inner peace, a quiet liberation, and a renewed sense of themselves as luminous beings beyond disease.

Lisa's journey helped her connect with a sense of empowerment, helping her recognize there was a certain power in being able to choose to let go. She said she felt like it was a choice that would be hers to make when she was ready. She was able to reflect on the ways in which she was still people-pleasing by battling through all the cancer treatments that were wearing her out. She recognized that ultimately a time would come when she could make the choice to let go of the battle, of doing it for others, and of her time in her physical body.

> She experienced in her journey a deep knowing that leaving her body would not be an ending but the beginning of a different journey.

She saw and felt a beauty and peace that awaited in the meadow beyond. That experience quieted the grip of her fear and opened her to peace beyond the pain. She cried and grieved for the time she would not get to spend with her husband and sons, but her soul had spoken to her heart, and she trusted that her next journey would be the one that would lead her home.

As each woman shared her journey, the group's connections deepened. It was easy to see and feel the medicine that was present in the act of holding space and witnessing each other.

I am always humbled by the beautiful healing elements of connection, compassion, and empathy present in these soulful retreats. Retreats and group work invite a strong medicine that is often overlooked in clinical and therapeutic models: connection as medicine.

To bring more awareness to the power of women supporting each other through cancer with plant medicine, this retreat was made into a beautiful documentary titled *Last Journey*. Lisa and the other women gave this project their blessing, and I am ever so grateful to them all for the amazing strength and vulnerability they were willing to share on camera.

A few months after this retreat, Lisa crossed over into the light. It was not easy for her to let go, but her journey helped her travel a bit more lightly to that crossing. It opened a door to a new perspective on her path and allowed her to glimpse the light beyond.

USING PSILOCYBIN WHEN FACING A TERMINAL DIAGNOSIS

Research on psilocybin-assisted therapy shows proof and the potential of psilocybin in helping women with cancer confront and ease the fear of death. Clinical trials at institutions like Johns Hopkins and NYU have demonstrated that a single high-dose psilocybin session, in a supportive therapeutic setting, can significantly reduce anxiety, depression, and existential distress in patients facing life-threatening illnesses, including cancer.[24]

INTEGRATION PRACTICES FOR ACCEPTING DEATH

Integrating a psilocybin experience to ease end-of-life and existential distress is a vital part of the healing process. While the medicine journey can offer profound insights and emotional release, it is the thoughtful integration afterward that helps those insights take root and create lasting peace. For women facing cancer or terminal illness, integration can support acceptance, connection, and a reframing of death not as an end, but as a meaningful transition. These practices can help anchor the transformation, allowing you to live more fully and die more peacefully—with dignity, presence, and love. Lisa found peace and a level of soul healing by moving mindfully though her end-of-life journey.

Here are some integration activities that may be especially helpful.

- **Nature Immersion:** Spending time in quiet natural settings can deepen the sense of connection experienced during the journey and soothe the nervous system. Nature reminds us of the cycles and seasons of death and rebirth.

- **Legacy Journaling:** Writing letters to loved ones, or documenting personal wisdom and life reflections, can bring meaning and closure.

- **Creative Expression:** Painting, collage, or poetry can help you process emotions and give shape to ineffable spiritual insights. For example, Lisa painted an image of the beautiful meadow she saw, showered in light, with birds circling above.

- **Ritual and Ceremony:** Creating a personal ritual to honor the life lived and the life still unfolding can bring peace and sacredness to the remaining time. Lisa had her husband find her a piece of dented, rusted metal, and she used this as a symbol of the armor she wore and was ready to take off and let go.

Journaling Prompts

1. What did I feel or understand about death during my journey that I didn't before?

2. What unfinished emotional or relational work am I being called to tend to now?

3. What brings me a sense of peace or beauty in this moment, and how can I make space for more of it?

4. If I were to leave a message to those I love most, what would I want them to know?

5. How has this experience changed how I want to live the rest of my life, no matter how long I have?

6. Where do I believe my soul was before I was born? Where do I believe my soul will journey to when I leave this existence as I know it?

CHAPTER 11

The Portal to Awakening Wisdom and Healing

> Women are the medicine the world has been waiting for.
>
> — SHAKTI GAWAIN

Throughout these pages, you have witnessed the stories of women who stepped bravely into the unknown—journeys through grief and awakening, fear and forgiveness, and ultimately transformation. Guided by psilocybin as a portal, they touch the deep well of their inner wisdom. Yet these stories are not only about psychedelic journeys. They speak to the universal currents that shape all of our lives—the soul's longing for wholeness, the body's ancient capacity to mend and renew, and the spirit's unshakable desire to remember who we truly are.

Psilocybin may open doors to profound mystical experiences, but the mystical is not bound to medicine alone. It lives in the thresholds of our everyday existence—in the first breath and the final exhale, in heartbreak and wonder, in dreams and stillness, in the wild places where the Earth herself speaks. We are built for transcendence. It is etched into our biology and woven into our spiritual inheritance. Often it rises in the raw, liminal moments of life—when love breaks us open, when loss strips us bare, when illness humbles us, or when awe reminds us of mystery. These are the portals that call us home.

This book has invited you to see how psilocybin journeys can help us navigate life's hardest passages. Whether facing the weight of catastrophic illness or grieving the unimaginable loss of a child, mushrooms can serve as companions, helping us access the wisdom and healing that already live within us.

The stories here also remind us of a vital truth: the importance of set and setting. Without the right mindset or environment, a psilocybin journey can become disorienting and difficult, without direction, rather than healing. With the right conditions, however, the same journey can open into clarity, compassion, and peace.

Equally essential is the presence of skilled support—a trained psychedelic guide, sitter, or facilitator who can hold the container with steadiness and care. Ideally, your guide will offer thoughtful preparation, including a consultation and screening process that helps you clarify your intention for this work. Trust is the foundation. Whoever you choose to walk with you, take time to build a relationship of safety and respect before entering such a deep inner landscape.

THE GREAT REMEMBERING

As women, we are natural mystics. We feel deeply, sense intuitively, and carry an embodied wisdom passed down through generations. An invisible, yet undeniable, web—emotional, energetic, and soulful—connects us. When plant medicine enters this space, it doesn't give you something you do not have; it awakens in you the things you have forgotten. It clears the static, softens the armor, and invites you back to your original knowing.

> The psilocybin renaissance is not just a cultural or medical shift; it is a spiritual homecoming.

We are not meant to walk this life path alone. Like the mycelium beneath the forest floor—quietly connecting root to root, tree to tree—we too are part of a vast unseen network of healing and wisdom. Each journey is personal, but the ripple effects impact us all. A collective consciousness is growing. There is an awakening of women and women's wisdom—and psilocybin is eager to support us in our remembering and returning.

This is the moment where science and soul meet. Where medicine meets magic. Where ancient knowing and modern wisdom weave together. Where everyone's healing is part of the collective healing. And where the magic—real and rooted—begins.

Let this book not be an ending but an initiation and invitation. A calling to keep listening, keep feeling, and keep awakening—to the wisdom within and the magic all around.

We are all the medicine. We are all the magic. We are all remembering! And the journey has only just begun.

ABOUT THE AUTHOR

Heather A. Lee, LCSW, is one of the nation's first certified and licensed psychedelic-assisted psychotherapists and has devoted over 30 years to helping people heal and grow as a licensed clinical therapist. With training from the Harvard Mind/Body Medical Institute and a background as the coordinator of Midlife Women's Health Education at the University of Virginia Medical Center, Heather has long been a leader at the intersection of psychology, women's wellness, and mind-body medicine.

As founder of Medicine Woman Retreats, she has guided hundreds of women in safe, legal psilocybin experiences across the globe. A pioneer in bringing psilocybin to women over the age of 60,

Heather inspires women in midlife and beyond to embrace this new season as a time of vitality, wisdom, and transformation. Her retreats, teachings, and international speaking engagements have positioned her as a trusted voice in the psychedelic renaissance, especially for women navigating aging, loss, or life transitions.

Heather's passion is creating communities of conscious women who support one another while stepping into their deepest wisdom and power. Her groundbreaking work has been featured in national media and documentaries, and at global conferences. When not leading retreats or speaking, she finds joy in nature, travel, and soulful connections.

ACKNOWLEDGMENTS

I must start with gratitude for Joy, my mother and greatest support. I count myself among the lucky girls who "drew a good mom card." My mother had the blessing of having a strong and loving mom herself (my Little Grammy), and that lineage of strength, care, and wisdom has been passed down woman to woman, generation to generation. The power of strong women raising strong women is the foundation upon which I stand. That solid footing allowed me to learn to trust myself, step into my own voice, and follow my own path and passions. Watching my entrepreneurial mother build a business that not only filled homes with beautiful handmade crafts but also nourished hearts with her listening ear and wise counsel showed me that work could be both art and heart.

So much gratitude for my daughters, who inspire me every day to live life to its fullest and with the most beautiful authenticity. It is a great pleasure to cheer their accomplishments and serve as a role model for them, showing them the magic of manifesting our dreams. And I share the warmest of appreciation and love for my husband Tom, who is the president of my fan club and always believes in me, even when I doubt myself. His steady love and consistent support mean so much to me.

I owe special gratitude to my college professor Dr. Barbour, who pulled me aside in my senior year and told me I was one of his brightest students and that I should pursue a master's degree. I had never considered myself to be master's degree material, but his words in that moment were like the Wizard of Oz handing me the diploma that reminded me of my own wisdom that I had possessed all along.

I am also thankful for my hippie college friends who, in my freshman year, introduced me to mushrooms not as a party drug but as a spiritual path—an introduction that quietly planted a seed that would blossom decades later into the work I now do. I am grateful also to the indigenous students at Arizona State University, who welcomed me as a graduate student to cofacilitate their campus support group and shared their beautiful traditions with me and our circle.

Each of these encounters and each of these people has helped open the portal that led me to my perfect path and passionate profession. Above all, I am ever grateful to the beautiful women who entrust me to hold space for their journeys. It is the deepest honor of my life, and the connection we share in that sacred space holds a magic beyond what words can capture, a mystery that continues to humble and inspire me.

GLOSSARY

For those just beginning to explore psychedelic psychotherapy, here's a simple introduction to some key terms and concepts.

Harm Reduction refers to the supportive presence of a trained sitter or guide to support you during your personal use of psilocybin.

Heroic Dose (Macro Dose) Five grams of natural mushrooms in the form of a tea is the typical amount used by certified facilitators. The guide or sitter ensures safety and emotional support while allowing the journey to unfold without interference.

Integration is a vital part of any psilocybin experience or session. During this period, you work with your therapist to reframe old memories, practice new emotional responses, and lean in to new narratives about your life and your path. With guidance, you revisit past events using therapeutic tools like parts work, somatic regulation, and trauma-informed narrative reprocessing. Integration therapy during this time involves intentionally rewiring the brain and reinforcing an identity rooted in healing, wholeness, and personal choice.

Journey refers to the altered state of consciousness entered when psilocybin is consumed, most often as a warm mushroom tea, followed by four to six hours of inner exploration. Journeys can take place in various settings—private one-on-one sessions, harm-reduction sitting experiences, or immersive retreat environments.

Each offers a different way to engage with the medicine, but all open the door to non-ordinary states of consciousness.

Macro Dose typically indicates ingesting three grams or more of psilocybin, which induces an altered state of consciousness.

Microdose (Microdosing) involves taking a very small, sub-perceptual dose of psilocybin, typically a fraction (perhaps one-tenth) of a gram. While you don't experience any psychedelic effects while microdosing, it can gently enhance neuroplasticity, the brain's ability to form new neural connections. This state of cognitive and emotional flexibility can support personal growth, creativity, and mental wellbeing.

Neuroplasticity is the brain's capacity to reorganize itself by forming new neural pathways. Psilocybin has been shown to temporarily boost this capacity, helping individuals shift out of rigid mental patterns and into more open, adaptive ways of thinking and feeling.

Plant Medicine refers to the therapeutic, spiritual, and healing use of plants and fungi—such as herbs, roots, leaves, seeds, and psilocybin mushrooms—that contain natural compounds capable of supporting physical, emotional, or spiritual wellbeing. Across cultures and throughout history, plant medicines have been used in rituals, traditional healing systems, and modern integrative health practices to alleviate illness, expand consciousness, restore balance, and connect people to nature.

Psilocybin is a naturally occurring psychoactive compound found in certain species of mushrooms, often referred to as "magic mushrooms." When ingested, psilocybin is metabolized in the body to psilocin, a substance that interacts with serotonin receptors in the brain, leading to altered states of consciousness. These effects may include changes in perception, mood, and thought patterns, and may create a sense of expanded awareness.

Psychedelic Medicine refers to the therapeutic use of psychedelic substances—such as psilocybin (from certain mushrooms), MDMA, LSD, ketamine, and ayahuasca—within a structured, intentional, and often clinically guided setting to support healing, psychological growth, and wellbeing. Unlike with recreational use, psychedelic medicine is practiced with preparation, guidance, and integration, often in psychotherapy or ceremonial contexts. Research shows it can help reduce depression, anxiety, post-traumatic stress, existential distress, and addiction; enhance self-awareness and emotional resilience; and provide a sense of meaning or spiritual connection.

Psychedelic-Assisted Psychotherapy (also referred to as Natural Medicine Facilitator) involves working with a trained facilitator or therapist before, during, and after a psilocybin session. Preparation helps clarify intention and foster trust. The session itself is guided in a safe and structured way, and integration supports making meaning of the experience afterward. In the US, both Oregon and Colorado have regulated models through the state for the licensing of therapists and psychedelic healing centers.

Set refers to your mindset and emotional state going into a journey. Feeling safe and supported and trusting your guide are essential. Having an intention for embarking on your journey is a crucial aspect of being prepared.

Setting refers to the physical environment where the session takes place. You should choose a location that feels safe, soothing, and free from interruptions.

APPENDIX

CONSIDERATIONS FOR YOUR PSILOCYBIN MEDICINE JOURNEY

SETTING DISTINCTIONS

Here are some considerations to help you choose between a group psilocybin retreat or a private psilocybin session with a qualified therapist.

Retreats offer a beautiful communal way for women to experience this medicine and these transformations together. Serene natural locations are ideal retreat settings. I have held soulful retreats—designed almost exclusively for women over 50—in Mexico, Costa Rica, and Portugal. Retreats vary, of course, but mine typically last between four and six days. The evening of our arrival, we gather over dinner to speak of our intentions as we weave together as a community. The next morning, everyone gathers for the journey ceremony to drink their mushroom tea. Each woman then goes to her own room or space to journey privately. The next few days of a retreat are filled with sound baths, yoga, nature immersion, and art activities designed to help participants integrate profound transformations from the medicine experience.

Private psilocybin sessions or psilocybin-assisted therapy sessions offer a one-on-one experience and include one or more preparation sessions to help you build trust in your facilitator and bring clarity to your intention. A therapist, facilitator, or sitter will be with you during the four to six hours of your journey. Afterward, you should expect to have one or more integration sessions to help you make sense of the experience and learn to work with your newfound wisdom.

⚠ IMPORTANT SAFETY & LEGAL CONSIDERATIONS

Used judiciously, psilocybin is generally very safe. The key to this medicine's safety is using it intentionally and seeking support from a skilled facilitator, guide, or therapist.

Psilocybin is not appropriate for everyone. It can be contraindicated for individuals with a personal or family history of psychotic disorders (such as schizophrenia or schizoaffective disorder), Bipolar I disorder, or certain untreated mental health conditions. Caution is also advised for those with serious cardiovascular disease, as psilocybin can temporarily increase blood pressure and heart rate.

Psilocybin may interact with psychiatric medications—particularly SSRIs, MAOIs, antipsychotics, and mood stabilizers—as well as other substances. For this reason, anyone considering psilocybin should be **screened by a qualified professional** trained in mental health assessment and knowledgeable about medication interactions and psychedelic therapy.

Psychedelic experiences can be powerful and destabilizing if undertaken without proper preparation, guidance, and support. Always approach with respect, caution, and professional oversight.

LEGAL ACCESS

In 2018, the US Food and Drug Administration designated psilocybin as a 'breakthrough therapy,' allowing research and studies into its treatment potential. This has led to rapidly changing regulations regarding its legal use. Currently, where psilocybin-assisted therapy is legal, it is only permitted to be used in approved treatment centers and administered by licensed professionals. Because legality and accessibility are changing rapidly in the US and across the globe, I encourage you to research the legal status of psilocybin mushrooms in your area.

ADDITIONAL RESOURCES

The following books, films, documentaries, and podcasts provide inspiring and practical perspectives on psychedelic therapy and the broader psychedelic renaissance. These resources are offered to inspire curiosity, deepen knowledge, and support your own journey of exploration. Always remember that psychedelic use should be approached with care and respect, and within legal frameworks.

BOOKS

Breaking Open the Head by Daniel Pinchbeck
A personal and cultural journey into psychedelics and shamanism.

High Priest by Timothy Leary
An autobiographical classic on Leary's early psilocybin research, including the Good Friday and Concord Prison experiments.

How to Change Your Mind by Michael Pollan
A landmark *New York Times* bestseller blending history, science, and memoir, exploring psychedelics' therapeutic potential.

Mindful Microdosing: A Guidebook and Journal
by Lauren Alderfer
A resource in which mindfulness meets microdosing to offer you a unique experience and unfolding process.

Philosophy of Psychedelics by Chris Letheby

An insightful look at psychedelic therapy through the lens of philosophy and neuroscience.

The Psilocybin Mushroom Bible by Virginia Haze and Dr. K. Mandrake
A comprehensive reference on psilocybin use, cultivation, and therapeutic applications.

The Psychedelic Explorer's Guide by James Fadiman
A trusted guide to safe and sacred approaches for exploring psychedelics.

FILMS AND DOCUMENTARIES

Dosed (2020)
A moving story of a woman's journey using psilocybin therapy to overcome addiction and depression.

Fantastic Fungi (2019)
A stunning visual exploration of the healing and ecological powers of fungi.

From Shock to Awe (2018)
Follows veterans healing from PTSD with psychedelics.

How to Change Your Mind (Netflix miniseries, 2022)
Four episodes inspired by Pollan's book, covering LSD, psilocybin, MDMA, and mescaline.

Last Journey (2025 Reason TV)
A powerful and soulful look inside a psilocybin retreat for three women with cancer, featuring Heather A. Lee.

Magic Medicine (2021)
Chronicles Imperial College London's groundbreaking psilocybin studies for depression.

Neurons to Nirvana: Understanding Psychedelic Medicines (2013)
Interviews with researchers and pioneers of psychedelic therapy.

A New Understanding: The Science of Psilocybin (2015)
Examines psilocybin's impact on easing end-of-life distress.

Psychedelia (2021)
Explores the mystical and cultural dimensions of psychedelic experiences.

PODCASTS

Mind Body Health & Politics (Dr. Richard Louis Miller)
A long-running series on mind-body medicine, psychedelic therapy, and social healing.

Mycopreneur Podcast (Dennis Walker)
Highlights innovators and entrepreneurs in mushroom culture and psychedelic wellness.

The Psychedelic Podcast (Third Wave)
Weekly conversations with leaders of the psychedelic renaissance.

Psychedelic Salon
Archiving voices of the psychedelic movement—researchers, elders, and psychonauts.

Psychedelic Somatic Interactional Psychotherapy
(Tamar Pearl and Jen Olson)
Focused on therapeutic frameworks for psychedelic-assisted healing.

Psychedelics Today
Deep dives into psychedelic science, culture, and therapy.

Truth Be Told with Tonya Mosley
Season 5 explores psychedelics as tools for healing racial trauma.

ENDNOTES

1. Griffiths, Roland R., Matthew W. Johnson, Michael A. Carducci, Annie Umbricht, William A. Richards, Brian D. Richards, Mary P. Cosimano, and Matthew A. Klinedinst. 2016. "Psilocybin Produces Substantial and Sustained Decreases in Depression and Anxiety in Patients with Life-Threatening Cancer: A Randomized Double-Blind Trial." *Journal of Psychopharmacology* 30 (12): 1181–97. https://doi.org/10.1177/0269881116675513.

2. Ross, Stephen, Anthony Bossis, Jeffrey Guss, Gabrielle Agin-Liebes, Tara Malone, Barry Cohen, Sara E. Mennenga, Alexander Belser, Kalliope Kalliontzi, James Babb, Zhenyu Su, Patricia Corby, and Brian L. Schmidt. 2016. "Rapid and Sustained Symptom Reduction Following Psilocybin Treatment for Anxiety and Depression in Patients with Life-Threatening Cancer: A Randomized Controlled Trial." *Journal of Psychopharmacology* 30 (12): 1165–80. https://doi.org/10.1177/0269881116675512.

3. Agin-Liebes, Gabrielle, Tara Malone, Mary M. Yalch, Sara E. Mennenga, Katherine L. Ponté, Jeffrey Guss, Anthony Bossis, Brian L. Schmidt, and Stephen Ross. 2020. "Long-Term Follow-Up of Psilocybin-Assisted Psychotherapy for Psychiatric and Existential Distress in Patients with Life-Threatening Cancer." *Journal of Psychopharmacology* 34 (2): 155–66. https://doi.org/10.1177/0269881119897615.

4. Mathis, Maria Alice de, Pedro de Alvarenga, Guilherme Funaro, Ricardo Cezar Torresan, Ivanil Moraes, Albina Rodrigues Torres, Monica L. Zilberman, and Ana Gabriela Hounie. 2011. "Gender Differences in Obsessive-Compulsive Disorder: A Literature Review." *Revista Brasileira de Psiquiatria* 33 (4): 390–99. https://doi.org/10.1590/S1516-44462011000400014.

5. Uguz, Faruk, Mine Sahingoz, Kazim Gezginc, and Rengin Karatayli. 2010. "Obsessive–Compulsive Disorder in Postmenopausal Women: Prevalence, Clinical Features, and Comorbidity." Australian & New Zealand Journal of Psychiatry. 44 (2): 183-87. doi:10.3109/00048670903393639

6. O'Connor, Sorcha, Kate Godfrey, Sara Reed, Joseph Peill, Cyrus Rohani-Shukla, Mairead Healy, Trevor Robbins, Ana Frota Lisboa Pereira de Souza,

Robin Tyacke, Maria Papasyrou, Dea Stenbæk, Pedro Castro-Rodrigues, Martina Chiera, Hakjun Lee, Jonny Martell, Robin Carhart-Harris, Luca Pellegrini, Naomi A. Fineberg, David Nutt, and David Erritzoe. 2025. "Study Protocol for 'PsilOCD: A Pharmacological Challenge Study Evaluating the Effects of the 5-HT2A Agonist Psilocybin on the Neurocognitive and Clinical Correlates of Compulsivity'." *Cureus* 17 (1): e78171. https://doi.org/10.7759/cureus.78171.

7   Moreno, Francisco A., Christopher B. Wiegand, E. Keolani Taitano, and Pedro L. Delgado. 2006. "Safety, Tolerability, and Efficacy of Psilocybin in 9 Patients with Obsessive-Compulsive Disorder." *Journal of Clinical Psychiatry* 67 (11): 1735–40. https://doi.org/10.4088/jcp.v67n1110.

8   Kelmendi, Benjamin, Alex Belser, Bradford Martins, Brian Zaboski, Christopher Pittenger, Helen Pushkarskaya, John Krystal, Jordan Sloshower, and Robert Rosenheck, and Terence Ching. 2025. "Efficacy of Psilocybin in OCD: A Double-Blind, Placebo-Controlled Study." Yale University, Yale School of Medicine. Last updated July 3, 2025. https://medicine.yale.edu/trial/neural-correlates-of-the-effects-of-psilocybin-in-obsessive-compulsive-disorder/.

9   Olff, Miranda. 2017. "Sex and Gender Differences in Post-Traumatic Stress Disorder: An Update." *European Journal of Psychotraumatology* 8 (Supplement 4): 1351204. https://doi.org/10.1080/20008198.2017.1351204.

10 Kraehenmann, Rainer, Katrin H. Preller, Milan Scheidegger, Thomas Pokorny, Oliver G. Bosch, Erich Seifritz, and Franz X. Vollenweider. 2015. "Psilocybin-Induced Decrease in Amygdala Reactivity Correlates with Enhanced Positive Mood in Healthy Volunteers." *Biological Psychiatry* 78 (8): 572–81.

11 Agin-Liebes, Gabrielle, Elizabeth M. Nielson, Michael Zingman, Katherine Kim, Alexandra Haas, Lindsey T. Owens, Ursula Rogers, and Michael Bogenschutz. 2024. "Reports of Self-Compassion and Affect Regulation in Psilocybin-Assisted Therapy for Alcohol Use Disorder: An Interpretive Phenomenological Analysis." *Psychology of Addictive Behaviors* 38 (1): 101–13. https://doi.org/10.1037/adb0000935.

12 McGowan, Niall M., James J. Rucker, Rachel Yehuda, Manish Agrawal, Nadav Liam Modlin, Hollie Simmons, Agata Tofil-Kaluza, Shriya Das, and Guy M. Goodwin. 2017. "Investigating the Safety and Tolerability of Single-Dose Psilocybin for Post-Traumatic Stress Disorder: A Nonrandomized Open-Label Clinical Trial." *Journal of Psychopharmacology*. https://doi.org/10.1177/02698811251362390.

Endnotes

13 Schwartz, Richard. 1987. "Our Multiple Selves: Applying Systems Thinking to the Inner Family." *Family Therapy Networker* 11 (2): 24–31.

14 Card, Kiffer G., Ashmita Grewal, Kalysha Closson, Gina Martin, Laura Baracaldo, Sandra Allison, Daniel J. Kruger, and Zach Walsh. 2024. "Therapeutic Potential of Psilocybin for Treating Psychological Distress among Survivors of Adverse Childhood Experiences: Evidence on Acceptability and Potential Efficacy of Psilocybin Use." *Journal of Psychoactive Drugs* 56 (5): 616–26. https://doi.org/10.1080/02791072.2023.2268640.

15 Basile, Kathleen C., Sharon G. Smith, Marcie-jo Kresnow, Srijana Khatiwada, and Ruth W. Leemis. 2022. *The National Intimate Partner and Sexual Violence Survey: 2016/2017 Report on Sexual Violence*. National Center for Injury Prevention and Control, Centers for Disease Control and Prevention.

16 Griffiths, Roland R., William A. Richards, Una McCann, and Robert Jesse. 2006. "Psilocybin Can Occasion Mystical-Type Experiences Having Substantial and Sustained Personal Meaning and Spiritual Significance." *Psychopharmacology* 187 (3): 268–83.

17 Garnett, Matthew F., and Arialdi M. Miniño. "Drug Overdose Deaths in the United States, 2003–2023." 2024. NCHS Data Brief, no 522. Hyattsville, MD: National Center for Health Statistics. doi: https://dx.doi.org/10.15620/cdc/170565

18 Ehrenkranz, Rebecca. Manish Agrawal, Kim Penberthy, and David Bryce Yaden. "Narrative Review of the Potential for Psychedelics to Treat Prolonged Grief Disorder." 2024. International Review of Psychiatry 36 (8): 879-90. doi:10.1080/09540261.2024.2357668

19 Low, Fiona, and Mitch Earleywine. 2024. "Psychedelic Experiences After Bereavement Improve Symptoms of Grief: The Influence of Emotional Breakthroughs and Challenging Experiences." *Journal of Psychoactive Drugs* 56 (3): 316–23. https://doi.org/10.1080/02791072.2023.2228303.

20 Ehrenkranz, Rebecca, Manish Agrawal, J. Kim Penberthy, and David B. Yaden. 2024. "Narrative Review of the Potential for Psychedelics to Treat Prolonged Grief Disorder." *Journal of Nervous and Mental Disease* 212 (12): 879–90. https://doi.org/10.1080/09540261.2024.2357668.

21 Beesley, Vanessa L., Tom J. Kennedy, Fiona Maccallum, Margaret Ross, Renee Harvey, Susan L. Rossell, Jerome Sarris, Daniel Perkins, Rachel E. Neale, James Bennett-Levy, Shevaugn Johnson, Hanna Beebe, Natalie Roset, Jörg Strobel, and Stephen Parker. 2025. "Psilocybin-

Assisted Supportive Psychotherapy in the Treatment of Prolonged Grief (PARTING) Trial: Protocol for an Open-Label Pilot Trial for Cancer-Related Bereavement." *BMJ Open* 15 (4): e095992. https://doi.org/10.1136/bmjopen-2024-095992.

22 Kurlander, Keith, host. 2020. "Learning About Psychedelics from One of the First Pioneers: Dr. Bill Richards HPP 61." *The Higher Practice Podcast for Optimal Mental Health*, August 19, 2020. 51:15. Integrative Psychiatry Institute. https://psychiatryinstitute.com/podcast/about-psychedelics-pioneers-richards/.

23 Carbonaro, Theresa M., Matthew P. Bradstreet, Frederick S. Barrett, Katherine A. MacLean, Robert Jesse, Matthew W. Johnson, and Roland R. Griffiths. 2016. "Survey Study of Challenging Experiences after Ingesting Psilocybin Mushrooms: Acute and Enduring Positive and Negative Consequences." *Journal of Psychopharmacology* 30 (12): 1268–78. https://doi.org/10.1177/0269881116662634.

24 Griffiths, Roland R., Matthew W. Johnson, Michael A. Carducci, Annie Umbricht, William A. Richards, Brian D. Richards, Mary P. Cosimano, and Margaret A. Klinedinst. 2016. "Psilocybin Produces Substantial and Sustained Decreases in Depression and Anxiety in Patients with Life-Threatening Cancer: A Randomized Double-Blind Trial." *Journal of Psychopharmacology* 30 (12). https://doi.org/10.1177/0269881116675513.

THANK YOU

Dear Reader,

I am so grateful that you picked up a copy of *The Psilocybin Sessions*. Your support means so much more than simply buying a book. It means you are curious about the growing circle of conscious seekers, courageous explorers, and soulful women reclaiming their wisdom and wonder. Each page was written with you in mind, so knowing that my words and these beautiful stories have found their way to you fills me with deep gratitude and joy.

As my gift to you, please download my free guided meditation at www.HeatherALee.com/Book.

If you feel called to explore psilocybin as a portal to your healing and transformation—whether through a private session, a soulful retreat, a weekend workshop, or an online gathering—I would love to connect with you. This is a time of great women's wisdom awakening, and it would be my honor to support you in stepping more fully into that through my current offerings at www.HeatherALee.com, including:

- **My Community Newsletter:** Be the first to know about all the fabulous events and gatherings we host and also get inspiring activities and tips for developing your intuition and inner wisdom.

- **Medicine Woman Retreats:** Transformative psilocybin and wellness retreats for women, held in beautiful locations around the world.

- **Private One-On-One Sessions:** Exclusive psilocybin sessions and mind-body wellness coaching for women over 50 exploring their inner wisdom for healing and personal growth; available in Colorado, Portugal, and the Netherlands.

- **Weekend Workshops & Online Gatherings:** Join the Conscious Conversation Collective—an online group that hosts global events designed to inspire intuition, deepen wisdom, and build a conscious community of women awakening together. Programs are held across the US, the EU, and online.

- **Speaking & Film Screenings:** Reach out through my website to ask about bringing me to your community or event as a speaker on women's wellness, psychedelics, or the wisdom journey. I also offer screenings and discussions with my documentary film *Last Journey*, which shares the soul-healing power of psilocybin for women with cancer and those at the end of life.

I look forward to meeting you and welcoming you into our growing circle of wise women.

With love and gratitude,
Heather

www.ingramcontent.com/pod-product-compliance
Lightning Source LLC
Chambersburg PA
CBHW060527080526
44586CB00012B/644